POEMS OF IVOR GURNEY
1890-1937

Photograph: Richard Hall

IVOR GURNEY

POEMS OF
IVOR GURNEY
1890-1937

With an Introduction by
EDMUND BLUNDEN

and a Bibliographical Note by
LEONARD CLARK

1973
CHATTO & WINDUS
LONDON

Published by
Chatto & Windus Ltd.
40 William IV Street
London W.C.2

*

Clarke, Irwin & Co. Ltd.
Toronto

ISBN 0 7011 1900 4

Introduction © Edmund Blunden 1954
Bibliographical Note © Leonard Clark 1973
Poems © Winifred Gurney, Dorothy Hayward
and Ethel Gurney 1917, 1919, 1954 and 1973

Printed in Great Britain by
T. & A. Constable Ltd.
Edinburgh

I would not rest till work came from my hand
And then as the thing grew, till fame came,
(But only in honour).

IVOR GURNEY
(In Dartford)

CONTENTS

*

OF ONE WHO SANG HIS POEMS

Long since, after the weary war, you came,
You, with a friend, to see me, and to sing
Poems of yours and ballads of old fame
Many a moving, many a merry thing.

I thought of Blake, the English lad who sang
To tunes too beautiful for tongue to tell,
Of Allingham, whose country ballads rang
Where Irish brooks, a winding river swell . . .

And of old poets, long-forgotten now,
Who, after singing, left, in country ears,
Notes that were comfort in the time of tears,
Words that directed furrows at the plough.

Themselves, perhaps, but memory of a tone
Of mirth, of sadness, never heard again,
An unseen thing that like a fallen rain
Or vanished warmth, has kindled a thing sown.

JOHN MASEFIELD

INTRODUCTION

I N the current edition of Grove's great *Dictionary of Music and Musicians* and in other works of reference the name of Ivor Gurney, 1890-1937, is not overlooked. He is given his place because of his distinction as a songwriter, and the already extensive list of his published music together with the appreciations of some of his fellow composers at once illustrates the rightness of the inclusion. The catalogue of all Ivor Gurney's publications, however, discloses that this remarkable song-writer was also the author of two collections of poems, which in fact at one time drew plenty of intelligent attention to his literary personality and promise. The two small volumes were *Severn and Somme*, 1917, and *War's Embers*, 1919. By way of these books and the occasional appearance of poems by him in the *London Mercury* and other journals, Gurney became known and has never been completely forgotten as one of the young poets brought to light in the First World War. It may even be true that his name has signified something through his verse to some who were unaware of his musical capabilities.

It is rarer than might be thought to find in a man the twofold gift of Ivor Gurney. We may instance among Englishmen the Elizabethan doctor Thomas Campion, the eighteenth-century entertainer Charles Dibdin, and, a little hopefully, the experimental Gerard Manley Hopkins. William Blake, we read, sang his lyrics to his own melodies, but could not record those melodies. The words of Sir John Squire nevertheless remain apt: 'I have known composers with a fine literary sense and poets who loved music but could neither compose nor play. I have known no man save Gurney who had the double creative gift that Rossetti had in *his* two arts.' The time was when Gurney could exercise his faculties for literary and musical composition more or less together; at other periods the practical difficulties of his daily life reduced his chances of writing songs and other music, and when things stood thus he turned with full devotion and adventure to his poetical vocation. In the end, his writings in verse amounted to a varied collection, of which the two published volumes had given only a small part; the plain reasons for the obscurity which so long enveloped almost all the rest appear in the brief biography following. Ivor Gurney's life story as well as his work brings him into the company of the young poets of England whose brief histories divide our feelings among what is pathetic, tragic, admirable and vital.

Nobody in Gurney's family before him is known to have made a name. His father had a tailor's shop at Gloucester, where the poet was born on 28th August 1890, the second of four children; he was called Ivor Bertie at his mother's desire, and christened by the Rev. Alfred Cheeseman, who stood godfather to him. Canon Cheeseman took a truly godfatherly interest in the child and very early introduced him to English poetry, and prose too, in an excellent library, one of the kind which Victorian clergymen often had. Gurney's parents saw to it that he (and his brothers and sisters) had some opportunity for music; and in 1900 Ivor Gurney passed from the choir of All Saints' Church to that of Gloucester Cathedral. At the same time he was sent to the King's School,

> Under the shade of the great Tower
> Where pass the lofty and the wise.

Here he stayed happily for five years. Out of school he enjoyed many well-remembered hours with the family of F. W. Harvey, who was also to make quite a name during the war of 1914-1918 as one of the welcome representatives of Gloucestershire in English poetry.

At the Cathedral Gurney distinguished himself as a solo boy. When that time was over he was qualified to become assistant organist, and he played the organ in various churches besides; he attempted composition, he wrote (over the pen-name 'Dotted Crochet') in the *Gloucester Citizen* on musical questions. He assailed local conservatism in the programmes of the Three Choirs Festivals. There was nothing of the supposed habits of the aesthete about him, and he enjoyed cricket and played a fair game of football. Among his diversions one was the care-charming subject of Mr Harvey's *Ballade of River Sailing*.

> *The Dorothy* was very small: a boat
> Scarce any bigger than the sort one rows
> With oars!

and yet this was, to her two poetical sailors,

> the prettiest little craft that goes
> Up-stream from Framilode to Bollopool

The invincible love of his county which Gurney's experiences as a child and as a youth implanted may be said to have acted at length almost as a tyranny over his poetical character and range.

In 1911 Gurney won a scholarship for composition at the Royal College of Music in London, then under the direction of Sir Hubert

Parry, and was placed for that study under Sir Charles Stanford; one who knew him sums up, 'Lessons under Stanford, and even more the College itself under Parry, opened out a new world.' Because of something in his countenance, he was promptly called 'Schubert'. He was not a noteworthy verse-writer, although as musician he was soon writing his Elizabethan songs. These were composed in his dull lodgings at Fulham. He lived in poverty; yet this was comparatively a serene chapter in his life. Partly spent in musical London and partly in old homes and familiar country, it hastened by, and on a sudden the month of August, 1914, presented to Gurney as to many millions of Europeans a personal problem needing to be answered quickly. He soon succeeded, in spite of poor eyesight, in joining the Yeomanry and early in 1915, we may imagine with what satisfaction, he was transferred to a Territorial battalion (the 2nd-5th) of the Gloucester Regiment. After a year's training in England the battalion went to augment the British Expeditionary Force in France, and, as was usual with reinforcements in the summer of 1916, the 2nd-5th Gloucesters made their first appearance in the forward area between Armentières and Béthune.

Those who were in that region in the bewildering summer of 1916 remember, apart from the intervals of violent and profitless battle in the trench zone, the inexpressible loveliness and lure of the passing hour. The country close to the firing line was still only slightly harmed; its husbandry remained quietly perfect; its substantial half-industrial towns, friendly villages, lonely corners, field-side shrines, avenues, villas, brooks and canals, beneath blue and white skies, and in dewy midnights, were peace itself—and more than common peace to those front-line troops who found themselves alive and respited for a space. The inhabitants were going on their ways as placidly as if the war was a greater distance off than an hour's walk, and the ordered life of centuries of good sense could be seen all round. Add to this that Gurney—he had now been turned into a signaller—was sharing things with men of his own shire, in whom a like tradition and a similar ability were personified, and we may see how this passage of his life as a soldier became a deep delight to him. When we observe that with it were mingled the extreme horror and regretted futility of his battlefield days and nights, we apprehend the general force of the period as it fastened on his imagination; and this also became even a partial tyranny over his later poetry.

An infantry soldier in the ranks (or otherwise, for that matter) could not carry many books during the trench warfare. In 1916

Gurney's reading was such as came his way incidentally, except for the poems of Keats, Housman's *A Shropshire Lad*, and a few other treasures.

The war on the Western Front became vaster and uglier. Gurney saw and took his share in the winter extensions of the Somme battle; on 7th April 1917 he was wounded, and so at last he found himself for six weeks away from the front line—in hospital at Rouen. He had been writing poems, which one after another were sent to a friend in London. The friend urged him to make a book of them, assisted in arranging it, and wisely offered it to Messrs Sidgwick & Jackson; it was accepted. Thus, with *Severn and Somme*, Ivor Gurney reported 'present' among the war poets available to the common reader who included Robert Nichols, Robert Graves, Siegfried Sassoon and many others, Rupert Brooke having led the way. His book, no imitation of the others in the list, reached a second edition.

The author resumed his place with the 2nd-5th Gloucesters near Arras and duly marched away North and into the Passchendaele battle (opened on 31st July 1917, with huge ambition but in the rain). Gurney felt that this offensive was even more ghastly than the Somme. He was gassed on 22nd August and sent to hospital near Edinburgh. In 1918 Gurney passed through a period of exceptional misery as an inmate of a mental hospital at Warrington, but when through the urgings of friends and the interest of Sir Hubert Parry he had been moved to another establishment at St Albans (the poet Cowper preceded him in this ordeal) he recovered. He was, however, discharged from the army one month before the fighting stopped.

Now Gurney could, and in January 1919 he did, take up his scholarship at the Royal College of Music. For this new period he became the pupil of Dr Vaughan Williams. But it came to an end, and Gurney was not of a type suited to the fight for a livelihood in London, though he managed in some way to struggle along. Probably he could not have managed it but for the fund which some friends, headed by his illustrious teacher, raised among themselves, providing him with a weekly allowance. Ivor Gurney's second book of poems, *War's Embers*, came out in 1919. In London he figured among the young men of the musical and literary world, whose name was mentioned occasionally, but was elusive and followed his instincts, which were not in the least prudent or provident. His conversation, no matter how he neglected such dull matters as meals and editorial requests, was ardent, audacious and timeless. It was already burdened with melancholy, and 'acquainted with grief'.

At the same time it is to be recalled that he did not easily lose hold of his earlier means of happiness and inward triumph. His friend

John Haines, also one of Gloucestershire's poets, has depicted him: 'After the Peace Ivor Gurney strode over Gloucestershire, a fierce, tall stooping but athletic figure, with bushy eyebrows and most piercing eyes, a kind of combination of Don Quixote and D'Artagnan, gallant, intractable, kindly, ferocious, and distressingly lovable.' It was from this friend that Gurney borrowed the recently published poems of G. M. Hopkins, which taught him much about his own poetic method, although the impact of Edward Thomas's work has been still greater. To quote John Haines again: 'With blazing eyes, he would pour forth an endless stream of talk on the English country, or on English poetry from Chapman to Edward Thomas, full of pithy and often violent, but always acute and exciting criticism.' Indeed the talk of Gurney in 1921 was so tumultuous and sharp that a close observer might have thought it ominous.

In the late Christopher Hassall's biography of Sir Edward Marsh some account of what happened to Gurney in 1922 is given. Walter de la Mare, who understood his poetry and knew of his privations, submitted his case to Marsh, who did what he could in his usual way; first of all he made Gurney a present out of the fund which Rupert had left him to dispose of. Then Sir Edward responded to Gurney's none too easy request to find him employment in the Income Tax office at Gloucester. It was found, but Gurney was in no condition to keep it. He visited Marsh in Gray's Inn, and took some poems by his friend William Kerr for approval—which was given. Kerr, however, had soon to assist Gurney in a less welcome direction.

One of the English poets to whose songs Gurney had been making tunes was John Clare, whose fate it was to pass twenty-seven years in lunatic asylums and to die in that restraint; a like fate befell Ivor Gurney. His delusions, not at all (it is believed) dangerous to others but imperilling him, led to his being confined from September 1922, first at Barnwood House, Gloucester, and later—when his recovery was felt to be extremely improbable—in the City of London Mental Hospital at Dartford, in Kent. As in the instance of Clare again, Gurney's confinement on the ground of insanity meant in general his banishment from public attention and his modestly won reputation, although his musical compositions were now and then brought out, and his setting of A. E. Housman were acclaimed. Old friends, Dr Vaughan Williams, Dr Herbert Howells, Miss Marion Scott, paid him visits. In many letters to all sorts of people—but the letters were not posted—he appealed for 'rescue'; some bore American addresses; and in these queerly phrased petitions there was no mistaking the derangement which kept him where he was. He was smouldering with anger which had for him the dreadful and undeniable cause that he, a lover of England if ever one existed, had been flung into a trap by England the beloved. 'The earth had opened,' a worse crater than any in Flanders and Picardy, for this defender.

In this dejection he had recourse to his music, but that was not at all easy; it was in poetry that in the ordinary way he found the going better, and he wrote a multitude of poems, planning new volumes capably enough, yet never attaining coherence quite long enough. This was an old characteristic now unfortunately emphasized. But there was meaning flashing within his faltering schemes. For a time —it is difficult to date his papers precisely—Gurney gave himself up in particular to the full and circumstantial account of his war experiences, into which of course his remembered Gloucestershire occupations and pastimes were for ever inwoven. He saw himself as 'the first war poet', and as one who had been shamelessly and cruelly treated; the obsession needs little comment except that, so far as his reading went, and in the notion that he was a complete writer, Gurney might fairly claim to be writing in verse of the soldier on the Western Front with a solitary originality. He described the life of the infantryman, as the examples of a host of poems given in this book will show, in a subtle series of reminiscence, catching many details and tones which had combined in the quality of seasons and moments, anguish and relief never again to occur. The poems may be still defective, most of them may swerve into ultimate confusion with themes not quite assimilated, but to this day they express part of the Western Front secret of fifty years ago with distinctive, intimate, and imaginative quickness.

It is not a serious disadvantage, surely, that these poems here and there contain a place-name or a war-term which is now unfamiliar or obsolete, nor even that other wars have been and other soldiers have brilliantly observed their pictures and paradoxes. The manner of Gurney's writing is already that of one perceiving a local and limited experience as sharing in the mystery of 'never again', *nous n'irons plus*, and giving to the names of some Flanders farm or cluster of cottages the value of a legend. There is no need, we may decide, for his reader to look up the map of North-East France in order to find exactly where La Gorgue is, or to consult military authorities concerning Dead End or Crucifix Corner. Such places, if we at length visit them, are not the places Gurney knew once 'like a passion' and always had in mind; those exist only in his poems as 'part of the music he heard', as fragments of the dream of life which seemed to his forlorn self to pause, through the magic contrast, long enough to simulate the eternal.

Much else which Gurney wrote in the approaches of his mental illness, and after its manifest arrival, was striking in the display of his ever-springing response to life physical and intellectual. Had he been able to keep a quiet mind, at the point when the business of meeting the demands of society, plain necessity, and prosaic citizenship had to be stubbornly faced, his prospects as a poet of the universal sort, with much more to give than Gloucestershire alone or the 2nd-5th Gloucesters taught and inspired, were good. But the crisis defeated the soldier from the wars. His subsequent efforts to defy his adversities exhausted what power he retained; his clearness lost its edge, and his once shrewd, even if it might be harsh, decision of language slackened into murmuring. Gurney's later manuscripts themselves, it is readily seen, betray the inability of a mind, somewhat conscious of intended form and content as a whole, to deliver any more than a loose and blurred shadow of these. The decline of his power of writing lyrics, once so intense and never facile, was physically inevitable.

Yet this poet was incapable of not writing his own especial nature into whatever verse even the last years produced. He saw and reflected for himself, and had shaped for himself a diction and a metrical action which the inferior piece or the scrap left unfinished share with the best; the ancient and the modern were curiously mixed in him, for he had lived as a wanderer in both ages.

On 26th December 1937, Ivor Gurney died at Dartford. Consumption had claimed one more poet as its victim, but one thing had given him genuine pleasure in his last days. The quarterly publication *Music and Letters*, on the suggestion of Gerald Finzi, published a group of articles in honour of Ivor Gurney, as man, as poet, and as musician. Dated January 1938, the issue appeared a fortnight earlier. The state of Europe at the time was utterly unpropitious for such appeals to the public taste, but those who had not forgotten Gurney's poetry were pleased with the sign that their admiration was not misplaced, and confirmed in their feeling that the utterances of a mind so energetic, so delicate often in its use of strength, so devoted to honour and to divine art, would not die away however long the dark spell might hang over the name of the poet. Of all the tributes written to him, none perhaps went closer to the character of Ivor Gurney than the simple record, 'Music and poetry have always meant so much to Gurney that he is prepared to make any sacrifices for them, and often has been too absorbed to notice a sacrifice has been made'.

The resentment of Gurney, no longer young, against those whom he looked on as having dismissed him from the world of men embittered his closing years; the presence of many other people in his daily round imposed its weight upon his wayward different nature. It would be a happiness to discover many brighter moments in his story at this stage, and perhaps the visit of an unfailing friend late in 1937 with the news that a collection of his songs was to be published by the Oxford University Press was one such moment. Gurney commented, however, with sad sanity, 'It is too late.' He was buried in Twigworth Churchyard and his old friend and benefactor Canon Cheeseman read the burial service over him; in an address to the congregation the Canon said that Ivor Gurney was himself one of 'war's embers'. The horror of it quenched the fire in him.

It now remains to speak of his manuscript poems, which have been gathered and preserved by the friend whom he gained when he first went ('wearing a thick, dark blue Severn pilot's coat') to the Royal College of Music. This far-seeing friend was Miss Marion M. Scott. Some of these pieces of the years of seclusion were grouped by the author for publication volume by volume. 'Rewards of Wonder: Poems of Cotswold, France, London' is a title too good to lose. 'Poems to the States', 'Six Poems Of the States', 'Memories of Honour; Infantry Poems of the State of New York', belong to a mood in which Gurney tries to be another Whitman or 'a son of Walt'. The poem on New York begins,

> To all I know lies there, farm land, plough or green
> I cry, to the kindness of faces I have not seen,
> I, war poet, maker of verse and infinite song,
> Who by the right of comradeship gathered knowledge
> And by comradship had knowledge earned and known.

'Poems in Praise of Poets, Poems of States' were intended as another collection. Besides all these there are numerous verses which apparently never were assembled with any design of forming distinct volumes. The whole is a profusion of poetry, through which the selector moves with the usual difficulty that its allusions and interests are often iterated and paralleled, that the subject with which Gurney began many a poem winds into another, and possibly yet more, according to his favourite sequence of retrospects or thoughts.

Many of these unpublished poems, then, interesting and stirring as they might be if they stood by themselves, are in a sense variants of the same foundational poem; but to decide which of them are the prototypes or at any rate the strongest and most communicative of the essentials in his outlook is a puzzle. There is in turn little to choose between one and another, and the solution of the editorial puzzle appears to be to take examples in which the principal topic survives least entangled with one or two of the others always crowding upon Gurney's memory. The constant regret which attends on the reading of these later poems is that the author's poetical resources and idea of poetry are felt to be decidedly greater than those he had in the days of his published volumes, but all is slowed down by an afflicting incoherence; we must accept the confusion continuing between imaginative purpose and the solace of merely enumerating as much as possible what had happened to the writer in times of comparative liberty. To resort to every gleam of remembrance for some humble comfort was natural to one in Gurney's situation and is observable in other ill-starred poets, in Christopher Smart and in John Clare, too; their best things when they were incarcerated necessarily took their rise from things past; but Gurney in his turn is even more strongly drawn away from the actual than those geniuses by his passion for what once was. His poems from his 'prison' too rarely reveal the new observation and fascination which brightened some of those written by Clare, when he was a mental patient at Epping and afterwards at Northampton. Clare was among Gurney's singers in words before his own doom was settled.

However that may be, it may not be fruitless to give a short description of one of his manuscript volumes—and I take for the sake of example a solid exercise book which he has filled up quite systematically. The title-page at once reveals, if anything can, the opposition between sense and delusion (if that is the right word) in his mind: it stands thus,

FIRST POEM

O what will you turn out, book, to be?
Who are not my joy, but my escape from the worst
And most accurst of my woe? Shall you be poetry,
Or tell truth, or be of past things the tale rehearsed?

'The book of Five makings'

Feb. 1925
(in torture)

Ivor Gurney

On the end page he writes a self-examination.

There is nothing for my Poetry, who was the child of joy,
But to work out in verse crazes of my untold pain;
In verse which shall recall the rightness of a former day.

And of Beauty, that has command of many gods; in vain
Have I written, imploring your help, you have let destroy
A servant of yours, by evil men birth better at once had slain.

And for my Country, God knows my heart, and men to me
Were dear there, I was friend also of every look of sun or rain;
It has betrayed as evil women wantonly a man their toy.

Soldier's praise I had earned having suffered soldier's pain
And the great honour of song in the battle's first gray show—
Honour was bound to me save—mine most dreadfully slain.

Rapt heart, once, hills I wandered alone; joy was comrade there
    though
Little of what I needed, was in my power; again—again
Hours I recall, dazed with pain like a still weight set to my woe.

Blood, birth, long remembrance, my County all these have saven
Little of my being from dreadfullest hurt, the old gods have no
Pity—or long ago I should have not good, they would have battled my
    high right plain.

I. B. G.

Between the preliminary and final verses the poet writes with
retrospection as his haunting mood, and it takes him alike to
Gloucestershire and to the provincial France he had seen in war; it
recurs occasionally to the London of his broken hopes. If he gets
free from these soliloquies about his experiences, he tries a straight-
forward poem on a general subject, the Elizabethans it may be, or
the palm willow, or (again the broad comparison with John Clare
is obvious) a dead child. He lives partly in his books, with his English
and French poets. During his occasional leave-days from the hospital
Gurney would make his way to the bookshops as of old. Sometimes
he revises with firmness, but as the collection grows he appears to
lose the artistic detachment and concentration implied in such care.
The lyrical outflash is rarer now; the inclination is meditative, con-
versational, and so the versification itself goes, sometimes grows
clogged almost completely. But the poet's eagerness will take its
turn, as in the discussion of 'the lost things' of Elizabethan dramatic
poetry:

What! not to outdo 'Cataline'—not write 'Hamlet' more fine?
Is Webster alone to surprise with beauty the soul of the eyes?
All honour to master, must we always serve George Chapman?
Or follow with love the nobility of John Marston?

It is remembered that even in his better situation Gurney was
passionately moved by the new discoveries (surely Dr Hotson's) on
Marlowe's cruel death. Everywhere the pages of the MS. book described gleam with the personal force of their writer, but the confident

light is intermittent, and in the end the chief effect is that of fits and starts of autobiography in need of excision and governed relationship.

From considerations like these it can be concluded that Gurney's abundant poetical remains offer plenty of possible selections, and that any one of those will create after all practically the same impression and bring the same report of the whole tantalizing legacy:

> The splendid fragments of a mind immortal
> With rubbish mixed, and glittering in the dust.

It is a mind of many faculties, adventurous and to some extent scholarly, observant and visionary, terse but desultory too, musical away from music itself, pictorial in expanses and in minuteness. The most eloquent observations on the range of Gurney's poetry, and he may have read them with refreshment of spirit if he had still strength to dwell on the printed word, are those of Walter de la Mare in 1937: let us borrow some of these. 'If he were a painter as well as a poet, he would be a master of skies and clouds. . . . He delights in an endearing particularity, refuses abstractions. . . . So, too, he always names his villages; rejoices in racy and well-seasoned words. . . . The paramount effect on the mind after reading these new poems is a sense of supreme abundance. One has ascended to the top, as it were, of some old Gloucestershire church tower, and surveyed in a wide circuit all that lies beneath it. And then, as with the reader of *The Dynasts*, one sinks unjarred to earth again; and all that is now so close and precise reveals why the distant seemed so lively, so lovely, and brimful of grace.'

Not much will be said here on the history of Gurney's poetics, or what is called technique, and on the influences which may have been important in it. He is often enough telling us of the authors in whom he delighted, and no doubt the indebtedness of this poet to Campion and to Carlyle, to A. E. Housman and to Edward Thomas, to American literature and to French will be investigated in course of time. The main truth concerning his way of writing is that he possessed from early days a peculiar unconventionality, not a quality hostile to traditions, but a view and a hearing of his own; and in poetics the masters of remote date or recent did not supply him with what he had not got, but energized his calls upon innate and personal strength. Gurney's 'gnarled' style was not that of Hopkins or of Bridges (who did not always write translucencies), but when he found such poets achieving their victories over the flying moment with strenuous remodellings of language, he was reassured and newly animated in his own search for the shrewdly different in phrasing and in metring. Probably much of his style is consonant with the first stages of his quick sensibility awakening among ancient buildings, especially country churches; he grew up with the instances of old craftmanship in carved work, stone or wood, ever in view and in reach. His poetry has its sweetness but it has sharpness and severity, or what he calls 'patterns like earth-sense strong'—something of the high-poised gargoyle against the flying cloud. It may have derived some of its uncommon melody from the wild tune of nature in the woods and waves, and some from the elder church music in which Gurney was proficient even as a boy. Whatever was attractive and poetically moving to the generation of writers called Georgians was so to him also, and he was content to be of that generation; but neither pussy-cat sentiment nor an indifferent 'eye on the object' can be imputed to him, nor yet trivial languor nor studied homeliness of expression. He perished, one may say, war and consumption apart, from the merciless intensity of his spirit both in watching the forms of things moving apace in the stream of change and in hammering out poetic forms that should remain as their just representation and acclamation.

EDMUND BLUNDEN

BIBLIOGRAPHICAL NOTE

Ivor Bertie Gurney, born in Gloucester on 28th August 1890, died in the City of London Mental Hospital at Dartford, in Kent, on 26th December 1937. He has long been recognized as a composer of songs which have enriched English music, and sufficient in themselves to ensure his immortality. He poured out these songs, of which nearly one hundred have been published, setting words by Elizabethan, and his own contemporary 'Georgian', poets.

But Ivor Gurney was also a practising poet who during his lifetime published two collections of verse, *Severn and Somme*, in 1917, when serving as a soldier in France, and *War's Embers*, in 1919, (both by Sidgwick & Jackson), when he had returned as a student to the Royal College of Music. These books focused further attention on him and on the rare double talent he possessed. But while the songs continue to be sung, the poems are virtually unknown, and the vast majority of them are unpublished. Yet even a casual reading reveals a poetic gift of a high order, unusual in its imaginative power, intense passion and originality. A more critical examination, both of individual poems, and of his work as a whole, suggests that Ivor Gurney should be considered one of the most important of the First World War poets. Certainly he had a greater range of feeling and intensity, and of personal involvement, than many of the 'established' war poets of that generation. That war laid particularly grim fingers on Ivor Gurney. Had there been no war he might have remained a charming regional poet; instead he became charged with a horror and misery which were to remain with him to the end of his miserably unhappy days. The war stretched him, because he was the kind of man he was, to a point where stretching had no more meaning, and in so doing gave a keener edge to his acute vision and also fundamentally affected and substantially changed his poetic technique.

As far as is known there are 880 poems in existence, written between 1913 and 1937. It is likely that he wrote many more, for it was his habit to send poems to friends, and he had little sense of order and rarely kept copies of his original manuscripts. Although a large number of his letters remain, there are few poems written in his own hand: 880 poems in twenty-four years is in the nature of a major output, especially when it is remembered that of these twenty-four years, Gurney spent four in the army and fifteen in lunatic asylums.

Yet both these periods bore poetic fruit, partly because the conditions made the writing of music much more difficult. Forty-six of these poems were published in *Severn and Somme*, 58 in *War's Embers*, and 78 in *Poems by Ivor Gurney*, selected from his unpublished work, and with a memoir, by Edmund Blunden, which was published by Messrs Hutchinson in 1954. There remain, therefore, 698 unpublished poems.

That any of Gurney's work survives at all is due almost entirely to Marion E. Scott of the Royal College of Music, who befriended him when he was a student there, and continued to champion his cause to the day of her death. Gurney regularly sent his poems to Miss Scott, who had them typed and returned to him, but who also kept carbon copies. It seems clear that she also returned the originals to him. It was Miss Scott who arranged for the publication of *Severn and Somme* and *War's Embers*, and it was she who, in 1918, sent some of his poems to Robert Bridges, then Poet Laureate, via Sir Charles Stanford. Bridges had admired earlier poems of Gurney's and told her that they had given him great pleasure. On 18th March of that year Bridges wrote to Stanford as follows:

'I have read Ivor Gurney's poems. I read them before I read his preface and came to the conclusion that he had certainly come in contact with the poems by Gerard Hopkins wh. I printed in "the Spirit of Man"—and I find in his preface that he had been reading that book.

'I thought that the best of his poems were the later sonnets in which this influence is evident. It seems to me that Gerard Hopkins' bold way of dealing with his thought suited Gurney very well—such verse as

"Only the love of comrades sweetens all,
Whose laughing spirit will not be out-done"

"Tho' Heaven be packed with joy bewildering
Pleasure of soul and heart and mind, yet who
would willingly let slip, freely let go
Earth's natal loveliness" —

'I thought that in these poems he had found a worthier expression than was at his command before, and shd he think of taking to writing poetry, he might wish to perfect his manner before he introduced himself to the public. On the other hand his liking for Hopkins points to his taste being *naturally* very severe and artistic, and in that case his earlier easier style might be more popular than his later would be.

'I am of course wholly in favour of the latter.

'The value of the poems as spontaneous statements of conditions of mind under strange conditions of present interest I do not feel called on to estimate. You would probably be able to judge of that better than I can.

'I shd. judge that it is certainly in his power to write good poetry if he gave himself up to it—and if that is so, then it follows that something of his natural artistic gift will appear in almost everything that he does either ill or well. How far this will affect the public and please them is more than I can guess. It seems a matter of chance.'

It remains a mystery why nothing more was done about the publication of Gurney's poems after 1919 when his powers had developed so considerably. Gurney sent poems to his close friends of Gloucestershire, John Haines, solicitor and man of letters, F. W. Harvey, the poet, and Herbert Howells, the musician. There was also Edward Marsh, who, to the disappointment of many, did not include any of Ivor Gurney's poems in his series of anthologies of Georgian poetry. It remained for another musician, Gerald Finzi, to do Gurney the greatest service of all. Though Finzi never knew him personally, he greatly admired his work as a song-writer and a poet, and it was he who assembled the greater part of Gurney's work and made possible the total number of poems. Finzi gathered them from every known source, including the files of the *R.C.M. Magazine*, the *London Mecury* and the *Gloucester Journal*; it was he who initiated the publication of the Blunden selection in 1954.

The chief sources of Gurney's unpublished poems are the note-books and collections in typescript now housed in the Gloucester Public Library.

1. *The Black Notebook* sent by Ivor Gurney to Herbert Howells between 1914 and 1917. Thirty-seven of the poems in *War's Embers* come from this book.

2. A notebook called *Songs from the 2/5th Gloucesters*. The poems in this are in the handwriting of an unknown friend.

3. A collection called *Rewards of Wonder: Poems of Cotswold, France, London*. This belongs to the period of 1919-1925.

4. *A little blue pocket book* belonging to the period 1919-1922 containing poems written while on a walking tour of Wales and the Welsh border with John Haines. These are poems written in the early days of his confinement.

5. Typescript poems called *Memories of Honour. Infantry Poems of the State of New York*. Dated 1925.

6. Typescript collection called *Poems to the States. Six Poems of the States*.

7. Typescript collection called *Poems in Praise of Poets. Poems of the States*.

8. A marbled notebook containing poems written in Dartford Asylum between 1922 and 1937.

The titles which mention the United States are of particular interest. Gurney was well versed in American literature and believed in the future of America as the great saving nation of the world. When in agony and desperation in Dartford, he wrote numerous letters to the States imploring people there to get him released from confinement.

It is not the purpose of this note to go into any detailed criticism of Gurney's poems. What the later work reveals is not so much a slackening of imaginative power or of the severe demands of poetic composition, but rather a change of style and a re-fashioning of technique as his ordeal made its slow, but inexorable, mark on his mind and spirit. There was no radical change of direction but a hot kindling, under torture, of what had always been a unique talent. He was compelled, during his asylum years, to write in the way he did because he had to speak out *somehow* or be cast into an even deeper hell of confusion and frustration. Poem after poem show how the words gushed out of him, as if he were some St Sebastian stricken in many places. There are numerous versions of several of the poems, and revisions which show that Gurney had many periods of lucidity. The tremendous stream of creation in him was never entirely silenced by the form of derangement from which he suffered, and which today might well be recognized in less black and white terms. This is not to deny that he was an extreme eccentric, the prey of grotesque illusions and, at times, of acute melancholia.

In all his writing Gurney was influenced by the Elizabethan poets and dramatists; he wanted to share with everybody his exultation in Shakespeare, Dekker, Marlowe and Jonson. But Ivor Gurney had his own individual style, which reflected his highly personal attitude to the world and to the things and people in it. This style might be described as 'knotty', or 'craggy', fascinatingly unconventional, often tortuous, sometimes as wild as the work of Christopher Smart. Gurney telescoped his thoughts so much that they are sometimes very difficult to unravel, the punctuation is often hopelessly misleading, and yet, the sense is always there, especially when the poems are read out loud. It is as well to remember that Gurney had a very acute ear for words and music. He possessed such an unusual imagination and ear, that technically, he is separated from many of his smoother Georgian contemporaries. Few poets have chosen such striking titles for their poems or explored such novel poetic territories. For Gurney, beauty and strangeness in all things was everything and it is this

30

adoration of the sublime which illumines many of his strange themes. His poems sing the praises of his country of Gloucestershire. They are full of his zest for Beethoven, Schubert and Bach. They reveal his admiration for America and France. They are inspired by the knowledge that the Romans had tramped over Cotswold and through Severn. There are love poems, too, in which Gurney reached out for a happiness which could not be granted to him. So much in his life was to be unrequited.

But it was his hatred of war and conflict which was to be his unrelenting protest. Although he valued the friendships which that war produced, and the moments of tranquillity which he enjoyed in the French countryside, there was nothing else about the war which was ennobling for him. He loathed its waste, despised its negativeness, was horrified by its squalor and bloodshed. He knew, before the war had ground itself to a miserable conclusion, that he was one of its embers, ruined forever by its fires. He may be compared, in part, to John Clare in that his confinement dragged some of the most poignant poems from him. The poems which he wrote 'behind the walls' are of unbearable agony, of a growing awareness that nothing could ever come right for him, that everything worth while would arrive too late for his enjoyment. Gurney's asylum poems, with their undertow of abject misery, are thunderbolts of rebellion rather than arrows of desire.

Ivor Gurney died on the anniversary of the martyrdom of St Stephen, Boxing Day, at the time of the year which meant a great deal to him though he saw it more as a period of death than of birth. In the asylum he turned for comfort and, perhaps, for guidance, to the dead and their spirits and wrote many odd and remarkable poems about those ghostly landmarks of the English year—All Hallows' E'en, All Souls' Day, St Martin's Tide, St Sylvester's Night.

The present selection of 139 poems from Ivor Gurney's work arranged as far as possible in chronological order, shows, if it shows anything at all, that it was not for nothing that he wrote a poem, in 1925, which had for its sub-title the words 'In torture', and which begins —

> There is nothing for my Poetry, who was the child of joy,
> But to work out in verse crazes of my untold pain;
> In verse which shall recall the rightness of a former day.
>
> And of Beauty, that has command of many gods; in vain
> Have I written, imploring your help, who have let destroy
> A servant of yours, by evil men birth better at once had slain.

Poetry which was 'the child of joy', worked out 'in verse crazes of my untold pain'. The poetry is in the agony rather than in the pity.

The pity is for Ivor Gurney himself whose generation did not know that he was burning and palpitating in their midst, with a fiery brain and heart, singing songs of the heart's pain and the world's loveliness, and hating what man's wars had done to man.

LEONARD CLARK

POEMS OF IVOR GURNEY

SONG OF PAIN*

Out of my sorrow have I made these songs,
    Out of my sorrow;
Though somewhat of the making's eager pain
    From Joy did borrow.

Some day, I trust God's purpose of Pain for me
    Shall be complete,
And then—to enter in the House of Joy . . .
    Prepare, my feet.

TO THE POET BEFORE BATTLE†

Now, youth, the hour of thy dread passion comes;
Thy lovely things must all be laid away;
And thou, as others, must face the riven day
Unstirred by rattle of the rolling drums
Or bugles' strident cry. When mere noise numbs
The sense of being, the fear-sick doth sway,
Remember thy great craft's honour, that they may say
Nothing in shame of poets. Then the crumbs
Of praise the little versemen joyed to take
Shall be forgotten; then they must know we are,
For all our skill in words, equal in might
And strong of mettle as those we honoured. Make
The name of poet terrible in just war,
And like a crown of honour upon the fight.

---

* *Severn and Somme*. Sidgwick & Jackson, 1917.
† 1. The *R.C.M. Magazine*, Vol 12, No. I, Christmas Term, 1915. 2. *Severn and Somme*, 1917. 3. Appeared in J. C. Squire's *Selection from Modern Poets*, Secker, 1921.

STRANGE SERVICE*

Little did I dream, England, that you bore me
Under the Cotswold hills beside the water meadows,
To do you dreadful service, here, beyond your borders
And your enfolding seas.

I was a dreamer ever, and bound to your dear service,
Meditating deep, I thought on your secret beauty,
As through a child's face one may see the clear spirit
Miraculously shining.

Your hills not only hills, but friends of mine and kindly,
Your tiny knolls and orchards hidden beside the river
Muddy and strongly-flowing, with shy and tiny streamlets
Safe in its bosom.

Now these are memories only, and your skies and rushy sky-pools
Fragile mirrors easily broken by moving airs . . .
In my deep heart for ever goes on your daily being,
And uses consecrate.

Think on me too, O Mother, who wrest my soul to serve you
In strange and fearful ways beyond your encircling waters;
None but you can know my heart, its tears and sacrifice;
None, but you, repay.

THE MOTHER*

We scar the earth with dreadful engin'ry;
She takes us to her bosom at the last;
Hiding our hate with love, who cannot see
Of any child the faults; and holds us fast.
We'll wait in quiet till our passion's past.

* *Severn and Somme*, 1917.

36

BACH AND THE SENTRY*

Watching the dark my spirit rose in flood
    On that most dearest Prelude of my delight.
The low-lying mist lifted its hood,
    The October stars showed nobly in clear night.

When I return, and to real music-making,
    And play that Prelude, how will it happen then?
Shall I feel as I felt, a sentry hardly waking,
    With a dull sense of No Man's Land again?

SONG*

Only the wanderer
    Knows England's graces,
Or can anew see clear
    Familiar faces.

And who loves joy as he
    That dwells in shadows?
Do not forget me quite,
    O Severn meadows.

* *Severn and Somme*, 1917.

AFTER-GLOW*
(*To F. W. Harvey*)

Out of the smoke and dust of the little room
With tea-talk loud and laughter of happy boys,
I passed into the dusk. Suddenly the noise
Ceased with a shock, left me alone in the gloom,
To wonder at the miracle hanging high
Tangled in twigs, the silver crescent clear—
Time passed from mind. Time died; and then we were
Once more at home together, you and I.

The elms with arms of love wrapped us in shade
Who watched the ecstatic West with one desire,
One soul unrapt; and still another fire
Consumed us, and our joy yet greater made:
That Bach should sing for us, mix us in one
The joy of firelight and the sunken sun.

PRAISE*

O friends of mine, if men mock at my name,
Say 'Children loved him.'
Since by that word you will have far removed him
From any bitter shame.

* *Severn and Somme*, 1917.

SONG OF PAIN AND BEAUTY*
(*To M.M.S.*)

O may these days of pain,
    These wasted-seeming days,
Somewhere reflower again
    With scent and savour of praise.
Draw out of memory all bitterness
    Of night with Thy Sun's rays.

And strengthen Thou in me
    The love of men here found,
And eager charity,
    That, out of difficult ground,
Spring like flowers in barren deserts, or
    Like light, or a lovely sound.

A simpler heart than mine
    Might have seen beauty clear
Where I could see no sign
    Of Thee, but only fear.
Strengthen me, make me to see Thy Beauty always
    In every happening here.

REQUIEM†

Pour out your light, O stars, and do not hold
    Your loveliest shining from earth's outworn shell —
Pure and cold your radiance, pure and cold
    My dead friend's face as well.

* 1. *R.C.M. Magazine*, No. 3, Vol. 13, Midsummer Term, 1917. 2. *Severn and Somme*, 1917. 3. Appeared also in J. C. Squire's *Selections from Modern Poets*. Secker, 1921.
† *Severn and Somme*, 1917.

THE OLD CITY (GLOUCESTER)*

Who says 'Gloucester' sees a tall
Fair fashioned shape of stone arise,
That changes with the changing skies
From joy to gloom funereal,
Then quick again to joy; and sees
Those four most ancient ways come in
To mix their folk and dust and din
With the keen scent of the sea-breeze.
Here Rome held sway for centuries;
Here Tomes Jones slept,
Here Rufus kept
His court, and here was Domesday born,
Here Hooper, Bishop, burned in scorn
While Mary watched his agonies.
Time out of mind these things were dreams,
Mere tales, not touching the quick sense,
Yet walking Gloucester History seems
A living thing and an intense.
For here and now I see the strength
In passing faces, that held at bay
Proud Rupert in an arrogant day
Till Essex' train bands came at length,
And King's Power passed like mist away.
Courage and wisdom that made good
Each tiny freedom, and withstood
The cunning or the strength of great
Unscrupulous Lords; and here, elate,
The spirit that sprang to height again
When Philip would conquer the wide Main
And England, and her tigerish queen.
Countenances here of antique grace
And beautiful smiling comedy look
That Shakespeare saw in his own place
And loved and fashioned into a book.
Beauty of sweet-blood generations
The strength of nations

* Written at Buire au Bois, July 1917.

Hear the passion-list of a fervent lover
The view from Over
Westgate Street at Night, great light, deep shadows,
The Severn meadows,
The surprising, the enormous Severn Plain
So wide, so fair
From Crickley seen on Coopers, my dear lane
That holds all lane-delightfulnesses there
(O Maisemore's darling way!)
Framelode, Frampton, Dymock, Minsterworth . . .
You are the flower of villages in all earth!
Whatever those may say
That have been cursed with an unlucky birth
Poor blinded multitudes
That far from happy woods,
Like these, in towns and hovels make their stay.
If one must die for England, Fate has given
Generously indeed for we have known
Before our time, the air and skies of Heaven
And Beauty more than common have been shown,
And with our last fight fought, our last strife striven
We shall enter unsurprised into our own.

MEMORY, LET ALL SLIP*

Memory, let all slip save what is sweet
Of Ypres plains.
Keep only autumn sunlight and the fleet
Clouds after rains.

Blue sky and mellow distance softly blue;
These only hold
Let I my panged grave share with you.
Else dead. Else cold.

* Written at Bangor, October 1917.

TO HIS LOVE*

He's gone, and all our plans
    Are useless indeed.
We'll walk no more on Cotswold
Where the sheep feed
    Quietly and take no heed.

His body that was so quick
    Is not as you
Knew it, on Severn river
    Under the blue
    Driving our small boat through.

You would not know him now . . .
    But still he died
Nobly, so cover him over
    With violets of pride
    Purple from Severn side.

Cover him, cover him soon!
    And with thick-set
Masses of memoried flowers —
    Hide that red wet
    Thing I must somehow forget.

* *War's Embers*, Sidgwick & Jackson, 1919.

DE PROFUNDIS*

If only this fear would leave me I could dream of Crickley Hill
  And a hundred thousand thoughts of home would visit my heart
                                                      in sleep;
But here the peace is shattered all day by the devil's will,
  And the guns bark night-long to spoil the velvet silence deep.

O who could think that once we drank in quiet inns and cool
  And saw brown oxen trooping the dry sands to slake
Their thirst at the river flowing, or plunged in a silver pool
  To shake the sleepy drowse off before well awake?

We are stale here, we are covered body and soul and mind
  With mire of the trenches, close clinging and foul,
We have left our old inheritance, our Paradise behind,
  And clarity is lost to us and cleanness of soul.

O blow here, you dusk-airs and breaths of half-light,
  And comfort despairs of your darlings that long
Night and day for sound of your bells, or a sight
  Of your tree-bordered lanes, land of blossom and song.

Autumn will be here soon, but the road of coloured leaves
  Is not for us, the up and down highway where go
Earth's pilgrims to wonder where Malvern upheaves
  That blue-emerald splendour under great clouds of snow.

Some day we'll fill in trenches, level the land and turn
  Once more joyful faces to the country where trees
Bear thickly for good drink, where strong sunsets burn
  Huge bonfires of glory—O God, send us peace!

Hard it is for men of moors or fens to endure
  Exile and hardship, or the Northland grey-drear;
But we of the rich plain of sweet airs and pure,
  Oh! Death would take so much from us, how should we not fear?

* *War's Embers*, 1919.

THE NEW POET

Out of the dark North and the easy South—
One with Saga strung against the bitter cold;
The other with happiness and homely songs of gold;
Let there be born a new poet—and let him sing
Of all the States, let his home be the Town watching
Mississippi flowing southward with names untold,
And water numberless hidden in Her flowing.
More honouring Masters old than one Walt Whitman,
Nor like Longfellow falling from his true matching
Of the nobility of earth with the nobility of words—
But out of Greece, Rome, Middle England and the all honouring
Provinces of France, and the Indian tradition,
A new poetry of all lights, all times; wherein swords
Are not honoured more than the shares ploughing
The coloured earth to furrows, dry or wet shards.
Let him say all men's thought nor sleep until
Some great thing he has fashioned of love inevitable.
For the rest, may he follow his happiness' true will.

CROCUS RING*

O show to me a crocus ring
That dances round a bush of green,
And I will make a lovely thing
To match the magic seen.

And swift the words should run to place,
The rhyming fall inevitable,
The crocus come to show its face
In sound set well.

* 1. Slightly different version published in *Music & Letters*, Vol. I, No. 4, October
1920. 2. This version in *Poems of Ivor Gurney*, 1954.

Children should read with bright-eyed wonder
And long to dance as flowers do,
Or fairies, in and out and under
Brambles and dew.

Clap hands and call for country going.
But O how false does memory
Play with a golden circlet growing
Round a March tree!

EQUAL MISTRESS*

Most tiny daisies are
Not anything
Less dear than the great star,
Riding the west afar,
To their Mistress Spring.

Jupiter, the Pleiades
To her equal
With celandine and cress,
Stone-crop, freckled pagles
And bird's-eye small.

Since in her heart of love
No rank is there
Nor degree aught; hers is
The most willing service
And free of care.

Violets, stars, birds
Wait on her smile, all
Too soon must Autumn come,
Sheaves, fruit be carried home,
And the leaves fall.

* *Music & Letters*, Vol. I, No. 4, October 1920.

WATER COLOURS

The trembling water glimpsed through dark tangle
Of late-month April's delicatest thorn,
One moment put the cuckoo-flower to scorn
Where its head hangs by sedges, Severn bank-full.
But dark water has a hundred fires on it;
As the sky changes it changes and ranges through
Sky colours and thorn colours, and more would do,
Were not the blossom truth so quick on it,
And Beauty brief in action as first dew.

THERE WAS SUCH BEAUTY*

There was such beauty in the dappled valley
As hurt the sight, as stabbed the heart to tears
And gathered loveliness of all the years
Hovered thereover, it seemed, eternally
Set for men's Joy. Town, tower, trees, river
Under a royal azure sky for ever
Up piled with snowy towering bulks of cloud
A herald-day of Spring more wonderful
Than her true own. Trumpets cried aloud
In sky, earth, blood; no beast, no clod so dull
But of the day, and of the giver
Was glad for life, humble at once and proud.
Kyrie Eleison, and Gloria,
Credo, Jubilate, Magnificat
The whole world gathered strength to praise the day.

* Written in pencil on a sheet out of manuscript book. Original given to M. M. S. by Ivor's mother, June 1939.

THE AWAKENING*

In the white painted dark lobby
The rosy firelight is thrown,
And the mat is still moisted with fresh mud
As I work at my task alone.

The murmuring of the kettle soothes me—
As those above sleep on still.
I love that dear winter-reflection . . .
Gone truant from loving too well.

COTSWOLD WAYS†

One comes across the strangest things in walks;
Fragments of Abbey tithe-barns fixed in modern
And Dutch-sort houses where the water baulks
Weired up, and brick kilns broken among fern,
Old troughs, great stone cisterns bishops might have blessed
Ceremonially, and worthy mounting-stones;
Black timber in red brick, queerly placed
Where Hill stone was looked for—and a manor's bones
Spied in the frame of some wisteria'd house
And mill-falls and sedge pools and Saxon faces
Stream-sources happened upon in unlikely places,
And Roman-looking hills of small degree
And the surprise of dignity of poplars
At a road end, or the white Cotswold scars,
Or sheets spread white against the hazel tree.
Strange the large difference of up Cotswold ways;

* Written in 1921 or 1922.
† 1. Published in a different version under the title of 'Encounters' in the *London Mercury*, Vol. VI, No. 36, October 1922. 2. Also appeared in J. C. Squire's *Younger Poets of Today*, Secker, 1922. 3. Published in *Poems of Ivor Gurney*, Hutchinson, 1954 under the title 'Cotswold Ways'.

Birdlip climbs bold and treeless to a bend,
Portway to dim wood-lengths without end,
And Crickley goes to cliffs are the crown of days.

OLD TUNES*

Out in the morning
For a speed of thought I went,
And a clear thought of scorning
For homekeeping: while downward bent
Grass blades with dewdrops
Heavy on those delicate
Sword shapes, wonder threat
Brightening my first hopes.

A four hour's tramping
With brisk blood flowing,
And life worth knowing
For all that something
Which let happiness then —
(Sometimes, not always,
Breath-on-mirror of days) —
And all gone now, since when?

* Written October, 1922.

THE SHAME*

If the pain I suffer were of the Devil enemy of Man
It might pass, might be proper, but from Man's self, O the
                                                    black shame
Of torture, when, as some think, so easy were the plan
Of kind life; but this is dreadfulness beyond name.

Each minute packed with a badness beyond words,
The brain, the mind tortured as blind stones would do,
What help in life? None. Hope is that Death affords
A shelter in some shade beyond Pain's come-through.

What help? Who tortures? and why? Why not grant Death
Which ends all, as some hope, and that Romans would think
An expiation complete; offence ended with breath
And self killing as good a deed as ever were drink.

TO GOD*

Why have You made life so intolerable
And set me between four walls, where I am able
Not to escape meals without prayer, for that is possible
Only by annoying an attendant. And tonight a sensual
Hell has been put on me, so that all has deserted me
And I am merely crying and trembling in heart
For Death, and cannot get it. And gone out is part
Of sanity. And there is dreadful Hell within me.
And nothing helps. Forced meals there have been and electricity
And weakening of sanity by influence
That's dreadful to endure. And there are orders
And I am praying for death, death, death,
And dreadful is the indrawing or out-breathing of breath
Because of the intolerable insults put on my whole soul,
Of the soul loathed, loathed, loathed of the soul.

* Written at Barnwood House, December 1922.

49

D

Gone out every bright thing from my mind.
All lost that ever God himself designed.
Not half can be written of cruelty of man, on man,
Not often such evil guessed as between Man and Man.

WALKING SONG

The miles go sliding by
Under my steady feet,
That make a leisurely
And still unbroken beat,
Through coppices that hear
Awhile, then lie as still
As though no traveller
Ever had climbed their hill.

My comrades are the small
Or dumb or singing birds,
Squirrels, field-things all
And placid drowsing herds.
Companions that I must
Greet for a while, then leave
Scattering the forward dust
From dawn to late of eve.

WHAT'S IN TIME*

What's in Time that it should frighten
The newborn child but just awoken
Out of some other life—from a woman's loins?
What's in Time, it should cry for its fear and pains?
The first pains, and the new breathing.
The strange coming to personality,
The growing boy, the mother leaving,
Insurrection and desire to be one's own and free.
The birth of creation in the heart, the touch of poetry.

'But these are not to be feared, they grow
Equal with use—as I and the world know!'
The coming to making and the finding the
Noblest string needs mastery.
The waking next morning to one's own scorning—
Dead leaves instead of the high unwondered tree.
To return, and labour and pain, and be
Broken by torture, in labour, to last effort.
And, the lover of God, be turned to smut
Because one man needed an evil gold;
And clean with hunger, dirted with eating,
Because some devil had mistaken in betting.
To make the time's greatest song, and be given
Dust on the covers for all the pain striven.
To cast out a shout of love to a far
Country, long loved, and be given bare
Silence, and cold unhonouring there.
'This is enough to break the heart
Of David the King set royal apart
The singer, the soldier, the maker of laws,
So he took Bathsheba to his hurt
And healed a heart-terror against cause
Of allowing.'
                    'True David had many sorrows,
Care hurt his forehead with lasting furrows.
I cured some bearing the fire and steel
Of a hundred cannons battering wheel against wheel,

* *Poems of Ivor Gurney*, 1954.

Battering huge violence down from the air,
With raining steel, and furious red fire
Hurtle of mass, Hell's insurrection furious.
Weight of unthought horror roused courage there.'

'You make me curious.'
'Yes, and the Death song men had waited
A thousand years for, and the all wanted
Hunger of home song write I in War . . . .
The song of a thousand years in passing,
And an ages song of home-despairing.
And lay in the darkness up against wires,
Watching the dark and the enemy's fires,
Feeling the bullets whizz past my tin helmet
(The Gloucesters impatient behind me) and set
Cold trembling fingers at order spoken
Against the damned wires, and to find them unbroken.
And to sing Home love at Caulaincourt.
To praise faith from Aubers to Ypres there,
And Wenlock Edge over Arras chalk looking.
To cough gas, and get recommended and be
Stopped of shoving by Richebourg, wading
Three feet of water past fire to the bones
For Hell cold east of snow-sleeting Chaulness,
Missed death, at Fauquissart, and St Julien —
Sniped to a hairs-breadth souvenir hunting
At Ypres — and frightened a hundred ways
Through all hours — of all summer and winter days.
'A soldier is all to be honoured surely?'

They gave me to Hell black torture as surely
As God — if He judge them shall judge for it.
They tortured my last nerve, and tortured my wit.
True later I wrote the noblest poem of Cities
And music the instinct of all the Pities
Tragedy, wonder, and of all home beauties
That Severn or Cotswold showed of their merely
Wonderful half-hour changes of watches
From Bredon to Berkely, and Crickley to Staunton —
Loveliest Country lost to all honoured Duties . . .
'But England's honour was assured of old blood

And sacrifice by Crecy and by Vermand wood . . .
Tears of poets, masters of music their gladness,
And if She turned, like this friend to madness
Scotland, Scotland surely would cry or hear her God!'

'I wrote Her best songs, and some verses.
I loved Her writers as men love their own born
Children from loins of love called for love's service.
And Ireland I loved like my heart's current.
Songs made I worthy of Aran or Narain Island,
Mused poetry with Synge, or with "Baile's Strand"
Made my thought fine when my own thought failed,
Heard Deirdre and Emir Conal call my command.
Ireland I loved, served Her as few have proved.
Tara, Connemara, Antrim, Mayo, left me
To be the easy prey of a Hell unaccountably
Let to the light free.'

'And Wales?'

'Welsh soldiers received us with tales
And songs, and courtesy like the Earth's and I
Have made Her great Song; and loved Her vales
And mountains, Her song and poetry—
Heard voices that mazed and that magicked me.'

The virtue is gone out of land and water
Houlihan's Daughter nor Britain's Daughter,
Nor Daughter of Gael, or West Severn lover
Have friended me, nor with steel nor freedom—
Past High God to most high God against me
Men have offended—their wives are whores
For their men's baseness not cast out of doors.
And the bastards born of their lust's embraces
Are hated of Hell for their concealing faces
Of shame better dead, and life better still,
A stuff of body lecherous from foul earth brought by will
Of evil to enact, or craft, or to endure all evil.
Cowards to live when Death cries to their courages . . . .
And the sacred separate Four-land honour of Islands—
The smut of vile branding their forehead brands.
Earth looks up, Heaven cowers to curse .

The water shrinks at them, the air with them withers.
Who leave a soldier, and a war poet,
A maker and lover, in Hell, for doubt
Whether Hell's evil is cured by Hell's repentance, or if
Their fathers with steel rose insurrections together
To risk a soul out of body so England
Should not have such dung guilt stuck to Her hand.
And ran upon Death so England should not be whored
By the lyingest devil, and lewdest with a word
Of anger — and no more, and rushed on any sword.

'You are in a temper.'
'I am.'
God curse for cowards; take honour and all damn
For bastards out of good blood, last leaving of diseases,
And rulers of England, lost in corruptions and increases
All mean, foul things they lap up like (powderless) jam —
While the cheated dead cry, unknowing, 'Eadem Semper'.

THE POETS OF MY COUNTY

One was a happy serious boy on lands
Of meadows — and went to France, and kept his hands
For bayonet readier than the pen, being likely
To dream into a poem men should not even see.
And one was sailor by Horn and Valparaiso, wrote
Such tale of Pompey as showed him rightly the great.
Another, the first, of St Thomas wrote imagining,
Of whom cuckoo flowers brought immortal lines and did sing
Like water of clear water — like April's spirit of Spring.
But what of Taylor, water-poet, who left desiring
The Roman town for the rich one, fame his heart so firing
He'd not heave cargoes nor draw wages by Severn?
And one wrote worthy verses indeed of the Four ways,
Coming in, watched of high clouds, for commercial days,
And military: another saw Ryton and wrote so —

Another yet wrote sonnets none so fool should forget.
(Of Rupert Brooke—gold winter on the sheets
Where light made memory of history of the room's happenings).
The love of Edward Thomas is nightwalkers promise.
But I praised Gloucester City as never before—and lay
By Tilleloy keeping spirit in soul with the way
Coopers comes over from Eastward sees Rome all the way.

ADVICE*

Why do you not steer straight, my love, she cried:
The wind makes steady your way, favours the tide:
The boat obeys the helm, were you now to steer
Courageous, our troubles and doubts would vanish here.

And cassia and pearls would pack your hold,
And your returning act crown manifold
Our upward course, and not a thing to desire . . .
The rudder swang in the tide, and we beached in the mire.

* The *London Mercury*, Vol. VIII, No. 43, May 1923.

ABOVE ASHLEWORTH

O does some blind fool now stand on my hill
To see how Ashleworth nestles by the river?
Where eyes and heart and soul may drink their fill.

The Cotswolds stand out Eastward as if never
A curve of them the hand of Time might change,
Beauty sleeps most confidently for ever.

The blind fool stands, his dull eyes free to range
Endlessly almost, and finds no word to say:
Not that the sense of wonder is too strange

Too great for speech. Naught touches him; the day
Blows its glad trumpets, breathes rich-odoured breath;
Glory after glory passes away.

(And I'm in France!) He looks, and sees beneath
The clouds in steady Severn silver and grey
But dead he is, and comfortable in Death.

STARS SLIDING

The stars are sliding wanton through trees,
    The sky is sliding steady over all.
Great Bear to Gemini will lose his place
    And Cygnus over world's brink slip and fall.

Follow-my-Leader's not so bad a game
    But were it Leap Frog: O! to see the shoots
And tracks of glory; Scorpions and Swans tame
    And Argo swarmed with Bulls and other brutes.

SONNET: SEPTEMBER 1922

Fierce indignation is best understood by those
Who have time or no fear, or a hope in its real good.
One loses it with a filed soul or in sentimental mood.
Anger is gone with sunset, or flows as flows
The water in easy mill rungs; the earth that ploughs
Forgets protestation in its turning, the rood
Prepares, considers, fulfils, and the poppy's blood
Makes new the old changing of the headland's brows.

But the toad under the harrow toadiness
Is known to forget, and even the butterfly
Has doubts of wisdom when that clanking thing goes by
And's not distressed. A twisted thing keeps still—
That thing easier twisted than a grocer's bill,
And no history of November keeps the guy.

CRUCIFIX CORNER

There was a water dump there, and regimental
Carts came every day to line up and fill full
Those rolling tanks with chlorinated clear mixture;
And curse the mud with vain veritable vexture.
Aveluy across the valley, billets, shacks, ruins,
With time and time a crump there to mark doings.
On New Year's Eve the marsh glowed tremulous
With rosy mist still holding late marvellous
Sun-glow, the air smelt home; the time breathed home.
Noel not put away; new term not yet come,
All things said 'Severn', the air was of those calm meadows;
Transport rattled somewhere in the southern shadows;
Stars that were not strange ruled the most quiet high
Arch of soft sky, starred and most grave to see, most high.
What should break that but gun-noise or last Trump?
But neither came. At sudden, with light jump

Clarinet sang into 'Hundred Pipers and A' ',
Aveluy's Scottish answered with pipers true call
'Happy we've been a' together.' When nothing
Stayed of war-weariness or winter's loathing,
Crackers with Christmas stockings hung in the heavens,
Gladness split discipline in sixes or sevens,
Hunger ebb'd magically mixed with strange leavens;
Forgotten, forgotten the hard time's true clothing,
And stars were happy to see Man making Fate plaything.

SMUDGY DAWN*

Smudgy dawn scarfed with military colours
Northward, and flowing wider like slow sea water,
Woke in lilac and elm and almost among garden flowers.
Birds a multitude; increasing as it made lighter.
Nothing but I moved by railings there; slept sweeter
Than kings the country folk in thatch or slate shade,
Peace had the grey West, fleece, clouds sure in its power,
Out on much-Severn I thought waves readied for laughter
And the fire-swinger promised behind elm pillars
A day worthy such beginning to come after.

Dawn came not surprising, but later widened
To great space and a sea of many colours
With slate and pink and blue above the frightened
Mud fields soiled and heavy with War's dolours—
And the guns thumped and threatened,
While the bacon frizzled, and the warm incense heightened,
Drifting in bays and dugouts slowly lightened.
First light bringing the thought what familiar star

* 1. The *London Mercury*, Vol. IX, No. 51, January 1924. 2. Appeared also, as two
poems, 'Smudgy Dawn' and 'Dawn' in J. C. Squire's *Selections from Modern Poets*,
2nd Series. Secker, 1929. 3. The single poem 'Smudgy Dawn' published in *Poems by
Ivor Gurney*, 1954.

There was, of town, farm, cottage, over there, over yonder,
And by day before duty settled awhile to
A companionship of good talk, forgetting night's woe.

THE CLOUD*

One could not see or think, the heat overcame one,
With a dazzle of square road to challenge and blind one,
No water was there, cow-parsley the only flower
Of all May's garland this torrid before summer hour,
And but one ploughman to break ten miles of solitariness.
No water, water to drink, stare at, the lovely clean grained one.

Where like a falcon on prey, shadow flung downward
Solid as gun-metal, the eyes sprang sunward
To salute the silver radiance of an Atlantic high
Prince of vapour required of the retinue
Continual changing of the outer-sea's flooding sun
Cloud royal, born called and ordered to domination,
Spring called him out of his tent in the azure of pleasure,
He girt his nobleness — and in slow pace went onward
A true monarch of air chosen to service and station;
And directed on duties of patrolling the considered blue.
But what his course required being fulfilled, what fancy
Of beyond-imagination did his power escape to
With raiment of blown silver . . . .

* 1. Slightly different version in The *London Mercury*, Vol. IX, No. 51, January 1924. 2. *Poems of Ivor Gurney*, 1959.

TOBACCO*

When tobacco came, when Raleigh did first bring
The unfabled herb; the plant of peace, the known king
Of comfort bringers, then indeed new hope
Came to the host of poets — with new scope,
New range of power, since henceforth one still might sit
Midnight — on and still further, while the war of wit
More kindly became and coloured till dawn came in;
Piercing blind shutter chinks with pale daylight thin,
Talk went on other things than the rich night did relate.

Raleigh he knew, but could not the impossible
War of swift steel and hurtled bronze foretell —
Nor the imaginary hurt on the body's vessel;
Nor how tobacco ever would steady disastered
Nerves, courage by gay terror almost mastered.
Gloucester men, half a day or more; they would hide
Five cigarettes and damp matches well inside
Their breasts, the only thing unsodded, while despair, despair
Dripped incessantly without interest from the air;
Or go supperless
The better next day's tobacco taste to bless.
Wonder at frogs, stars, posts till headaches came
Those chief of trouble-comforts still in number the same.
Watch Verey lights, sand-bags, grasses, rifle sights, mud —
Crampt in uncouth postures men crouched or stood —
A Woodbine breakfast inspiriting the blood.

Or in those caves of dugouts, men talking lazily
Smoke in luxuriously, of Woodbines, Goldflakes easily —
For one gift condoning Fate and its unnatural mazily
Self-tangled knots. Easing the strained back —
Somehow or other slipping unseen from the rack
Into tobacco scent, or tobacco savour or look;
The divine virtue of some content long-golden book
Multiplying; or in the sunniest quiet resting
Loll into restlessness or sleepy jesting.

* 1. Much shorter version appeared in the *London Mercury*, Vol, IX, No. 51, January
1924. 2. J. C. Squire's *Younger Poets of Today*, 1932. 3. This version in *Poems of Ivor
Gurney*, 1954.

Tobacco truly taken, as poetry, as a real thing.
Tobacco tasted exactly; in waves or odd ring
Noted; tobacco blown to the wind, or still watched
Melt into ether's farthest smother unmatched.
Keen sentries hid whiffing surreptitiously—
Sly fatigue parties hidden from scrutiny—
Last breath favours begged desperately.
Over all the breath of the airy vapour is known,
Life's curtain rises on it and Death's trembles down.
Heroism has taken smoke for sufficient crown.
Wires hang bodies for such courage as makes tobacco so known—
Machine guns sweep in heaps those who such honour keep.

When I think of the Ark slapping hopeless eternal waters—
Of Aeneas' sailors cursed with unclean hunger—
Or Irus and his scorn, or the legions Germanicus
Met, and was nearly scotted by whose just anger;
I know, I realize, and am driven to pity—
As by sunscorched eternal days of Babylon City—
And any unsoothed restless war people's clamour;
As hunger for Empire, any use of War's evil hammer;
Tea and tobacco after decent day body-clean labour,
Would bring again England of madrigal, pipe and tabor—
Merry England again of Daniel, after four centuries,
Of dawn rising and late talking, and go-as-you please.
But by Laventie or Ypres, or Arras the thing
Kept heart and soul together, and the mud out of thinking.
There was no end to the goodness, and Raleigh who journeyed
Far over waters to Virginia—and risked life and there did
Things like the heroes' things—but felt want never as we
Carefully guarding the fragments, and finishing the half spents—
Knew joy never so, nor pain; two hours and miles over sea.
How tell the poetic end and comfort of pain past any sustain?

SONG*

Past my window dawn and
    Through the open shutters thrown
Pass the birds the first awaking,
    And the light wind peace breaking.

Now the ink will dry on pen
    And the paper take no more
Thoughts of beauty from the far
    Night, or remembered day of men,
Cotswold breaking the dark or standing
    Brave as the sun, with white scar.

Now my footsteps shall go light
    By the fence and bridge till white
The farm show, that till now had glimmered,
    In the trees July had summered.

OLD TALE†

If one's heart is broken twenty times a day,
What easier thing to fling the bits away,
But still one gathers fragments, and looks for wire,
Or patches it up like some old bicycle tyre.

Bicycle tyres fare hardly on roads, but the heart
Has a longer time than rubber, they sheath a cart
With iron; so lumbering and slow my mind must be made—
To bother the heart and to teach things and learn it its trade.

* *Poems of Ivor Gurney*, 1954.
† The *London Mercury*, Vol. IX, No. 51, January 1924.

BRIMSCOMBE*

One lucky hour in middle of my tiredness
I came under the pines of the sheer steep
And saw the stars like steady candles gleam
Above and through; Brimscombe wrapped (past life) in sleep!
Such body weariness and ugliness
Had gone before, such tiredness to come on me
This perfect moment had such pure clemency
That it my memory has all coloured since,
Forgetting the blackness and pain so driven hence,
And the naked uplands from even bramble free,
That ringed-in hour of pines, stars and dark eminence;
(The thing we looked for in our fear of France.)

NEW YEAR'S EVE*

Aveluy and New Year's eve, and the time as tender
As if green buds grew. In the low West a slender
Streak of last orange. Guns mostly deadest still.
And a noise of limbers near, coming down the hill.
Nothing doing, nothing doing, and a screed to write,
Candles enough for books, a sleepy delight
And the warm dugout, day ended. Nine hours to the light
There now and then now, one nested down snug,
A head is enough to read by, and cover up with a rug.

Electric! Clarinet sang of a Hundred Pipers
(And hush-awe mystery vanishes like tapers
Of tobacco smoke), there was a great hilarity then.
Breath and a queer tube magicked sorrow from men.
Here was no soul's cheat, friends were of love over there—
How past thought, returning sweet! yet the soldier must dare.

* The *London Mercury*, Vol. IX, No. 51, January 1924.

THE SILENT ONE

Who died on the wires, and hung there, one of two—
Who for his hours of life had chattered through
Infinite lovely chatter of Bucks accent:
Yet faced unbroken wires; stepped over, and went
A noble fool, faithful to his stripes—and ended.
But I weak, hungry, and willing only for the chance
Of line—to fight in the line, lay down under unbroken
Wires, and saw the flashes and kept unshaken,
Till the politest voice—a finicking accent, said:
'Do you think you might crawl through there: there's a hole'
Darkness, shot at: I smiled, as politely replied—
'I'm afraid not, Sir.' There was no hole no way to be seen
Nothing but chance of death, after tearing of clothes
Kept flat, and watched the darkness, hearing bullets whizzing—
And thought of music—and swore deep heart's deep oaths
(Polite to God) and retreated and came on again,
Again retreated—and a second time faced the screen.

FIRST TIME IN

The Captain addressed us. After glow grew deeper,
Like England, like the West Country, and stars grew thicker.
In silence we left the billet, we found the hard roadway
In single file, jangling (silent) and on the gray
Chipped road, moaned over ever by snipers' shots.
Got shelter in the first trench; and the thud of boots
On duck-board wood from grate on rough road stone it changed.
(Verey lights showed ghastly, and a machine gun ranged).
Sentry here and there. How the trench wound now! Wires
Hindered, thistles pricked, but few guns spat their fires.
Upward a little . . . wider a little, the reserve line reached.
Tin hat shapes, dark body shapes and faces as bleached.
And the heart's beat: 'Here men are maimed and shot through,
                              hit through;

Here iron and lead rain, sandbags rent in two;
And the honours are earned. The stuff of tales is woven.'
Here were whispers of encouragement, about the cloven
Trenches faces showed and West soft somethings were said,
Lucky were signallers who (intellectual) strangely had
Some local independence in Line danger, but
In training or on Rest were from honour shut.
Bundling over sky lines to clear trench digging—
On the Plain scorn went with tapping and flag wagging
Directions. And then one took us courteously
Where a sheet lifted, and gold light cautiously
Streamed from an oilsheet slitted vertical into
Half light of May. We entered, took stranger-view
Of life as lived in the Line, the Line of war and Daily
Papers, dispatches, brave-soldier talks, the really, really
Truly Line; and these the heroes of story.

Never were quieter folk in teaparty history.
Never in 'Cranford', Trollope, even. And as it were, home
Closed round us. They told us lore, how and when did come
Minnewerfers and grenades from over there east;
The pleasant and unpleasant habits of the beast
That crafted and tore Europe. What line mending was
When guns centred and dugouts rocked in a haze
And hearing was difficult— (wires cut) —All necessary
Common sense workmanlike cautions of salutary
Wisdom—the mechanic day-lore of modern war-making,
Calm thought discovered in mind and body shaking.
The whole craft and business of bad occasion.
Talk turned personal, and to borders of two nations.
Gone out; Cotswold's Black Mountain edges against august
August after-suns glow, and air a lit dust
With motes and streams of gold. Wales her soul visible
Against all power West Heaven ever could flood full.
And of songs—the Slumber Song, and the soft Chant
So beautiful to which Rabelaisian songs were meant;
Of South and North Wales; and David of the White Rock:
What an evening! What a first time, what a shock
So rare of home-pleasure beyond measure
And always to Time's ending surely a treasure,

Since After-war so surely hurt, disappointed men
Who looked for the golden Age to come friendly again.
With inn evenings of meetings in warm glows,
Talk: coal and wood fire uttering rosy shows
With beer and 'Widdicombe Fair' and five mile homeward—
Moonlight lying thick on frost spangled fleet foot sward,
And owl crying out every short while his one evil word.

At any rate, disputeless the romantic evening was—
The night, the midnight; next day Fritz strafed at us,
And I lay belly upward to wonder: when—but useless.

CANADIANS

We marched, and saw a company of Canadians,
Their coats weighed eighty pounds at least, we saw them
Faces infinitely grimed in, with almost dead hands
Bent, slouching downwards to billets comfortless and dim.
Cave dwellers last of tribes they seemed, and a pity
Even from us just relieved, much as they were, left us
Lord, what a land of desolation, what iniquity
Of mere being, there of what youth that country bereft us;
Plagues of evil lay in Death's Valley we also
Had forded that up to the thighs in chill mud,
Gone for five days then any sign of life glow,
As the notched stumps or the gray clouds then we stood;
Dead past death from first hour and the needed mood
Of level pain shifting continually to and fro,
Saskatchewan, Ontario, Jack London ran in
My own mind; what in others? these men who finely
Perhaps had chosen danger for reckless and fine chance,
Fate had sent for suffering and dwelling obscenely
Vermin eaten, fed beastly, in vile ditches meanly.

SCHUBERT*

The loved one, in the great fiery mood, the not asking mood;
After a century still the greatly loved one;
But the true Celt in him wholly was undone
By his Fate; storms tossed him half out of his good.
One reads and loves the story of his short stay;
Early rising, Beethoven-following and the rest—
(Only the peasant wants our liking, quick maker, the guest
Of beer-drinkings)—he the player of pipes, of first day
The Lover, and of stars; true one, faithfullest and shyest.
One holds him but as part of what was to be,
Square shaper, bender of metal, happy in task.
The known figure in Vienna grows comradely
With five continents, and but great honour to ask—
Would Death take all too soon what was of Europe's own?
(Although lacking the greatness of the high maker's starkness.)
Yes, indeed, like Keats, Shelley, and the divine Mozart
Death cared no more for him or us than to break heart
With rape-of-beauty—hiding for ever under darkness
Mind of the 'Erl-King' and the East wind's hurt sighing;
The Unfinished Symphony—and a hundred things more of pride
Or natural truth. Since Marlowe or perhaps John Fountain died
Perhaps the world suffered never so—heart had not such denying.

BEETHOVEN†

Beethoven, I wronged thee undernoting thus
Thy dignity and worth; the overplus
Of one quartet would our book overweigh—
Almost chosen out at random from your own day.
You have our great Ben's mastery and a freer

* 1. *Music & Letters*, Vol. VI, No. 2, April 1925. 2. *Poems of Ivor Gurney*, 1954.
† 1. *Music & Letters*, Vol. VIII, No. 2, April 1927. 2. *Poems of Ivor Gurney*, 1954.

Carriage of method, spice of the open air . . . .
Which he, our greatest builder, had not so—
Not as his own at least but acquired to.
May no false fashion put thy true fame away
As in Vienna, when wantons laid all away
Thy work Homeric for a soft Southern zephyr,
And heroes were no other than as day's heifer
Sacrificed on the altar of world's praise,
The amusement or brittle heightening of drab days;
Whereas thy sinewed strength is by Aeschylus,
Homer, Ben Jonson, Shakespeare, and a pillar of us.
Master! Such are our memories which do never betray
Our own makings, thou so generous in thy great-heart way.

TEWKESBURY*

Some Dane looking out from the water-settlements,
If settlements there were, must have thought as I,
'Square stone should fill that bit of lower sky.
Were I a King and had such influence,
Farms should go up for this, flames make terror go high;
But I would set my name in high eminence.'
Forthampton walking, thinking, looking over to Tewkesbury,
Where a cricketer was born and a battle raged desperate,
And mustard grew, and Stratford boys early or late
May have come, and rivers—green Avon, brown Severn—meet.
And Norman Milo set a time's seal on the plain—
As, 'Here man rules; his works to be found here;
Acknowledges supremacy, his strength to be in vain;
And gathers by a sign the broad meadows in round here.'

* 1. The *Gloucester Journal*, 10th June 1951. 2. *Poems of Ivor Gurney*, 1954.

That is best of England, going quick from Beauty,
Is manifest, the slow spirit going straight on,
The dark intention corrected by eyes that see,
The somehow getting there, and last conception
Bettered, and something of one's own spirit outshown;
Grown as oaks grow; done as hard things are done.

NEAR VERMAND

Lying flat on my belly shivering in clutch-frost,
There was time to watch the stars, we had dug in:
Looking eastward over the low ridge; March scurried its blast
At our senses, no use either dying or struggling.
Low woods to left—(Cotswold her spinnies if ever)
Showed through snow flurries and the clearer star weather,
And nothing but chill and wonder lived in mind; nothing
But loathing and fine beauty, and wet loathed clothing.
Here were thoughts. Cold smothering and fire-desiring,
A day to follow like this or in the digging or wiring.
Worry in snow flurrying and lying flat, flesh the earth loathing.
I was the forward sentry and would be relieved
In a quarter or so, but nothing more better than to crouch
Low in the scraped holes and to have frozen and rocky couch—
To be by desperate home thoughts clutched at, and heart-grieved.
Was I ever there—a lit warm room and Bach, to search out sacred
Meaning; and to find no luck; and to take love as believed.

RIEZ BAILLEUL

Riez Bailleul in blue tea-time
Called back the Severn lanes, and roads
Where the small ash leaves lie, and floods
Of hawthorn leaves turned with night's rime,
No Severn though nor great valley clouds.

Now in the thought comparisons
Go with those here-and-there's and fancy
Sees on the china firelight dancy
The wall lit where the sofa runs.
A dear light like Sirius or Spring sun's.

But the trench thoughts will not go, tomorrow
Up to the line; and no straw laid
Soft for the body, and long nights dread
Lightless, all common human sorrow.
(Unploughed the grown field once was furrow.)

Meanwhile soft azure; the Falls' dusk clear
Lovely the road makes, a softness clings
Of colour and texture of light; there rings
Metal, as it were, in air, and the called
Of Twilight, dim stars of the dome appear.

So why muse more in the way of poet?
Lonely—when wine of estaminets
Was red to the spirit as to the gaze,
Golden the lamplight and boys who knew it,
Poets leave stars then, go human ways.

HALF DEAD

Half dead with sheer tiredness, wakened quick at night
With dysentry pangs, going blind among dim sleepers
And dazed into half dark, illness had its spite.
Head cleared, eyes saw; pangs and ill body-creepers
Stilled with the cold — the cold bringing me sane —
See there was Witcombe Steep as it were, but no beeches there.
Yet still clear flames of stars over the crest bare,
Mysterious glowing on the cloths of heaven.
Sirus or Mars or Argo's stars, and high the Sisters — the
                                        Pleiads — those seven.

Best turn in, fatigue party out at seven . . . .
What though beauty was — I had been Cranham's walks . . . .
Dark was the billet after that seeing of rare
Gold stars, stumbling among the still forms to my lair.
Still were the stars bright — my sick mind hung on them even.

But long after; in solitary day walking, I recalled
Caulaincourt's Mausoleum and the stars March midnight
                                        called;
On the east horizon's dim loveliest shape upheld.
To mix with music in my thought and forget sickness —
To drown sorrow deep that on me was then masterless —
Hunger and weak body and tired of needed sleep.
For Argo or Sirus in the East skies or for Regulus.

SERENADE

It was after the Somme, our line was quieter,
Wires mended, neither side daring attacker
Or aggressor to be — the guns equal, the wires a thick hedge,
When there sounded, (O past days for ever confounded!)
The tune of Schubert which belonged to days mathematical,
Effort of spirit bearing fruit worthy, actual.
The gramophone for an hour was my quiet's mocker,
Until I cried, 'Give us "Heldenleben", "Heldenleben".'

The Gloucesters cried out 'Strauss is our favourite wir haben
Sich geliebt'. So silence fell, Aubers front slept,
And the sentries an unsentimental silence kept.
True, the size of the rum ration was still a shocker
But at last over Aubers the majesty of the dawn's veil swept.

POET'S AFFECTION*

Reckoning good in time, how ruined and how fine the high poets
        stood
And seeing what I saw there, the blossoming meads of apple and pear,
        with rough bark-clothes wood,
I knew a thing not human killed the good of man and woman were it
        glory or straight making
Of fine eloquence or rhyme.
Then knew the high gods helpless save they took a power was
        dangerous
For aid for man his great plan fit to crown and traverse time.

Then all the men that walked there did I list in my thoughts,
Watching to hills and valleys that they listed for their pleasures
Made small symbols like rare treasures of, bediamonded rich small
        fraught
Their dawn looks and their day-falls from the North where Raphael
        Bredon falls
To Michael's hold, Crickley Nicholas Cooper's guard and glory,
Uriels English story and sway to valley of old that Randwich taught
Cried may the angels weakened care as much for England sickened
And the straightened poets beaten as those lovers for Severn's land's
Hollow hand. When the blackbird cried out 'Fealty to thee',
And the linnet, 'Obeisance, obeisance, O, Obeisance' from his tree.

Skylark, plover, rook, robin scarlet like a book
Wagtail shaking, making pointing joyous at first look,
Cried, 'Joy to thee, poets loved to be, may our service come to
        suffice to thee'.

        * Written in September 1926.

THE BATTLE

The Gloucesters were to go over I was not one—
Glad because of the terribleness, ashamed because of the terror,
I saw in the loveliest azure mist September had shown
Great spouts of white, heard thunders and knew that somewhere
Gloucesters were moving, men for three years I had known,
Perhaps to see no more—fallen from thought of their Shire
Even. High over all, guard on a machine gun,
Which yet might be needed (Doubt at Ypres the surer)
I saw blue mist and white smoke, but never fire,
Who heard two days after names I had sworn
Had long ago saved me—of men fallen by battle torn,
Whether alive or dead—I had sworn to their power.

HELLS PRAYER

My God, the wind is rising! on those edges
Of Cotswold dark glory might swing my soul—
And western Severn and North of water sedges
Mystery sounds. The wind's drums roll.
None will care to walk there. Those prefer to tell
Tales in a warm room of gossips, gettings, wages,
While I would be cursing exultant at the wind's toll
Of bell, shout of glory—swiftness of shadows.
My birth, my earning, my attained heritages,
Ninety tones denied me now thrust so far in Hell.

I think of the gods, all their old oaks and gages,
Gloucester has clear honour sworn without fail—
Companionship of meadows, high Cotwold ledges
Battered now tonight with huge wind-bursts and rages,
Flying moon glimpses like a shattered and flimsy sail—
In Hell, I buried a score—depth writing verse pages.

TO CRICKLEY

My soul goes there crying when
It is hurt by God far . . . .
It is hurt too far, and moves again
By green and quarry scar.

Ages and ages dreaming there
Speak their heart to me—
Generations of tried men honour
My broken good with pity.

'Such good' they say, your blood had
At birth, and in this
Land was given you music in mood
Noble, true, clamorous.

And what has broken England to such
Evil is not guessed
Nor those old sentries rustling grass rough
Know, nor the rest—

Soldier that knew war's pains, poet
That kept our love—
The gods have not saved you, it is not
Our prayers lacking to move.

Then to you—deep in Hells now still-burning
For sleep or the end's peace—
By tears we have not saved you; yearning
To accusation and our hopes loss turning.
What gods are these?

THE PLEASANCE WINDOW*

Now light dies from the pleasance
With rich look of colour
About the lawn, and winter
Whispers of leafless trees.

Of orange sunsets soft dying
And chill in the air at morning,
When friends will delight also
To speak of Artois' friends.

Warm straw after freezing ditches,
And soon will come long dark
Starry when the poet goes
Content, with his masters, out to stars.

BROWN EARTH LOOK

The youth burning couch grass is as tired
    As muscle has right to bear and keeps work on
And brown earth slopes from the potato field to the wired
    Sheep enclosure; and hidden high and white the sun.

Brown the sense of things, the light smoke blows across
    The field face, light blue wisps of sweet bitter reek
Dear to the Roman perhaps, so old seems the dross
    Burning of root, grass, wheat, so near, easy to seek.

Old is the land, a thousand more generations
    Have tilled there, sought with bright sweat the stuff of its
                     bread.
Here one comes for the sense of fine books, revelations
    Of beauty in usualty, found as well of heart as of head.

* Written 24/25 September 1926.

And all the tales of far Europe that come on one,
The sense of myriads tending the needings of life,
Are more to one than the near memory of battle guns
Peace with its sorrow blots out the agonies of strife.

YESTERDAY LOST

What things I have missed today, I know very well,
But the seeing of them each new time is miracle.
Nothing between Bredon and Dursley has
Any day yesterday's precise unpraised grace.
The changed light, or curve changed mistily
Coppice now bold cut yesterday's mystery,
A sense of mornings, once seen, for ever gone,
Its own for ever, alive, dead and my possession.

IMITATION

The door stands open
    Light is golden on the wall
Teatime is content within there
    Five o'clock winds call

Of summer, and the hot breath
    Is cooled of soaked air,
Afternoon rests after its strain
    Time moves steadier.

To a smooth going
    And flowing. Cottagers take
Content in thought of rested
    Strain, the evening is now a lake

Of gold all-too looked for. Meanwhile
  The Jubilee pictures are noted,
The blue and white china,
  And past summers are quoted.

Cottagers are happier now
  Than any perhaps
Of the townsfolk, tired
  Decent at hours' lapse.

Seeing as of right the true
  Texture of rare living
Azure had into nature, greed
  Tasted, thanked of the giving.

All common loveliest,
  Trifles apprehended,
Possessed, put aside then
  Garden calls, tea's ended.

While they must walk the Broadway
  Dusty, torrid with the Town sun,
And not knowing anything save
  The days' doing, the week done.

EAST WIND

Cool air moves there up on Cotswold edge,
By Crickley's bastion or the Shurdington wedge,
Gray grass rustles, the harebells dance and the East
Wind has no good influences on the cattle at feast.

Naked land-slides show, away down hill mist-shades cover
The land where South-west once moved high, like a lover
With colour and boy's glory and breath of renewal
That also, that valley for this dry air is a fuel.

But the great steeps keep one in right hoping still,
Mighty the upstanding curving of the golden-crowned hill—
See now, where scabious and the serious thistle nods,
And there is hiding place for the old gods.

LOOKING THERE

Out to the glow my eyes look from the writing place,
What glow there is is good after the blank and the ache
Of thinking in fields gone empty up into space,
And the wish for peace, the look for contentment's sake.
But I look for some past through the dear flames and remember
What thoughts were once known in bitter frost and—and
Loveliest light looked for in a coming December
Firelight, and after bright frost across the dark land.
Which after fulfilled in a longing for one companion,
Time gave for one minute, and snatched with a blackguard hand.
But there is no help is thinking past the deepest ache
Of heart, and empty in desire when the reach is far too far.
Tears cannot help the solitary one, the forgetting one, the self-
blinding one.
So if my thoughts hurt, I must leave my writing and go where
Stars and dusk may comfort my lost-souled despair,
And if not she, at least my Master Beethoven.
Are there not many ways for the heart to escape in loving?
And is the blood to be bright for one thought alone?
One quarter hour of moving and I shall forget all this.
If not, Ben Jonson: and the great surge and sway
Of 'Cataline' shall me save from the dangerous way
Of thinking of too much Beauty by an evil snatched
From one humble as David or as proud as Whitman,
Or glad as Pippa seeing the wide heavens unlatched . . . .
Misery drowns in many ways and I take this
To hurt a heart with making past remembrance—and to get
work done.

THE ESCAPE

I believe in the increasing of life whatever
    Leads to the seeing of small trifles,
Real, beautiful, is good, and an act never
    Is worthier than in freeing spirit that stifles
Under ingratitude's weight, nor is anything done
    Wiselier than the moving or breaking to sight
Of a thing hidden under by custom; revealed
    Fulfilled, used, (sound-fashioned) any way out to delight,
Trefoil — hedge sparrow — the stars on the edge at night.

THOMAS HEYWOOD

Thomas Heywood wrote his clerk's page each night,
Some guess, with a wary eye on it from winter's half-light
Or summer's thicker gold. But others must wonder
How such a slap-dash impulse could be so kept under
By willing mere putting-off. Where are his tavern scenes,
His gold-lit fire-embraced pictures of autumn dusk,
London quarrels, heath days where bowls played, inns and
                         the rest
Most prolific Heywood kept shut in his deep breast?
Head for gallery writing, hand put to his wine
Or fruit, Heywood the actor, friend of gentlemen fine.
Two hundred plays, that main finger; that clear writing
Would Fate have given him for smooth-tune inditing,
What desperate shifts drove him at whiles Lucrece
Must show, that horror clowned at, that Hell's jest so easy.

ON FOSCOMBE HILL

O, exquisite
And talking water, are you not more glad
To be sole daughter and one comfort bright
Of this small hill, lone-guarding its delight
Than unconsidered to be
Some waif of Cotswold or the Malvern height?
Your name a speck of glory in so many,
You are the silver of a dreaming mound
That likes the quiet way of thought and sound,
Moist tussocks with a sunken influence
Collects and runs one way down to farmyard
Sheds, house, standing up there by soft sward,
Green of thorn, green of sorrel and age-old heath
Of South-west's lovely breath.

SCHUBERT

Made the song as a slow movement
Of Beethoven, probably,
Took ordinary good health technique
Of Beethoven and used it against words,
When his mind was probably not up
To sustained flight or creative power.

The creation of the song is his great
Achievement, but there is at least
The 'Rosamunde Overture' and
'Unfinished Symphony' the 'Quartette
In D Minor', and as one says, the
'Quintette in C' which looks to have
Very good texture.

His work probably stands in fair
Relation to Burns, he having the same
Grip and peasant thought, but
Much more beauty. The
Amount of dull Schubert is vast.

LECKHAMPTON CHIMNEY
HAS FALLEN DOWN

Leckhampton chimney has fallen down,
The birds of Crickley have cried it—it is known in the town,
The cliffs have changed, what will come next to that Line
Watcher of West England, now that landmark has fallen.

Severn has changed course, it is known by Barrow;
Malvern may heave up in other lines by tomorrow,
But Maisemore Hill stable and rounded shall stay—
And strawberry flowers found surprise on Christmas Day.

Cleeve will front sunset, Birdlip shall have its road
Flung angled and noble on its breast broad.
Many things shall stay, but the stone Chimney,
Leckhampton's mark has fallen, like a stick or a tree.

AUTUMN'S FLAME

Autumn sent a flame
Up from the rough
Seven ages field for proof
Of her fine fame
On Cotswold in clear year-fall.

No music is there, no tongue
To tell the complete
Wonder surpassing great
Of the firs shape outflung
Against Cotswold Edge at the year-fall.

UP THERE

On Cotswold edge there is a field, and that
Grows thick with corn and speedwell and the mat
Of thistles, of the tall king; Rome lived there,
Some hurt centurion got his grant or tenure,
Built farm with fowls and pigstead and wood piles,
Waited for service custom between whiles.
The farmer ploughs up coins in the wet earth-time,
He sees them on the topple of crests' gleam,
Or run down furrow; and halts and does let them lie
Like a small black island in brown immensity,
Till his wonder is ceased, and his great hand picks up the penny.
Red pottery easy discovered, no searching needed . . .
One wonders what farms were like, (no searching needed).
As now the single kite hovering still
By the coppice there, level with the flat of the hill.

DARKNESS HAS
CHEATING SWIFTNESS

Darkness has cheating swiftness
When the eyes rove,
Opens and shuts in long avenues
That thought cannot prove.

Darkness shuts in and closes;
There are three ghosts
Different in one clump of hedge roses
And a threat in posts.

Until one tops the road crest,
Turns, sees the city lie
Long stretched out in bright sparkles of gratefullest
Homecalling array.

THE SEA BORDERS

Well I know though I have not seen how the white edges
Of the Sea make fury now by Devon or Maryland—
What grand spirit batters uselessly against old Brittany,
Or against Hebrides with black granite wedges
Of rock. And all the writers who ever have written the
Annals of seafaring will tell me little more
Of how the water at a huge ship's onset surges
Than my own little boat's prow sailing Severn recklessly.
(But O those great three masters of the past ages!)
Tales told in the foc'sle, or hauling hand over hand
Hauling on ropes, the companionship in close quarters—
The lovely shocks of beauty of the noises of broken waters . . .
These I have known, not because writers made tales to command
My shame and glory, and terror all clear to me.
Not because my life has had soldiership and greatest labour of body . . .
Not only because I musician have wrestled with the stuff in making,
And wrought a square thing out of my stubborn mind—
And gathered a huge surge of spirit as the great barriers bind
The whole Atlantic at them by Devon or West Ireland.

THE POET WALKING

I saw people
Thronging the streets
Where the Eastway with the old
Roman Wall meets—
But none though of old
Gloucester blood brought,
Loved so the City
As I—the poet unthought.
And I exulted there
To think that but one
Of all that City
Had pride or equity
Enough for the marvelling
At street and stone,
Or the age of Briton,
Dane, Roman, Elizabethan—
One grateful one—true child of that dear City
                                    —one worthy one.

THE COIN*

It is hard to guess tales at once from sight of a thing,
Suddenly brought to the light, though one may have blood
Of Rome, all instinct, and quick to the makers mood
So I could not tell, Constantine's coin, being up ploughed:
What manner of man had lost it, with what regretting,
And not till music began in my mind it seemed
Possible to find out from a heart that dreamed
Day long of Rome, majesty and mildness in setting
Of Crickley curves against Severn, and clouds that streamed.
So though it might have been the farmer that had lost,
Or mere private from the hillside missing beyond his cost

* One of two versions.

84

The Casualty let fall coin that not till now had gleamed
Above the shear of the plough, shown in the rubble of cutting.
Him I might have saluted, or round his shoulders
Put my arm—now could not be imagined, the horses' surges
Went up and down the field, Great bodies at strength held.
And the coin given me lay in my pocket, urges
Continual to take out the thing, and watch its so bold
Countenance of an Emperor, dust with all his friends that were,
But this symbol suddenly gathered from the many coloured
                                        mould.

FOR MERCY OF DEATH

I suffer racking pain all day, and desire Death so—
As few desire. Where is Man's mercy gone?
Did ever past generations such torment know
Who lived near Earth, and joyed when the sun shone,
Or when sweet rain came on
The earth; and the afterglow
Of sun and flowers in show
Of golden sweetness gladdened Earth's dear son?
Where is that mercy now
That palpably took pleasure in the sweep
Of hedgerows—high to deep—
And houses in the making; Man's own dear
Vesture and shelter here?
O sure it is that if those olden-time
Builders of farm and byre
Were here again, my pain should pity receive—
Death should make no more to grieve
My spirit with such pain it knows not how
To endure. O show
Such olden pity on poor souls in pain.
Let rest again—
As would our fathers friends of wind and rain.

THE DEARNESS OF COMMON THINGS

The dearness of common things,
Beech wood, tea, plate shelves,
And the whole family of crockery,
Woodaxes, blades, helves.

Ivory milk, earth's coffee,
The white face of books
And the touch, feel, smell of paper,
Latin's lovely looks.

Earth fine to handle,
The touch of clouds
When the imagined arm leaps out to caress
Grey worsted or wool clouds.

Wool, rope, cloth, old pipes
Gone warped in service
And the one herb of tobacco,
The herb of grace, the censer weed
Of blue whorls, finger-traced curves
The touch of sight here strange and marvellous
To any blind man pierced through his opaque,
When concrete objects grow.

ANDROMEDA OVER TEWKESBURY

Andromeda over Tewkesbury in state
Has taken place with calm and lucent mien,
I think the dark houses there have been
A hundred times so set, but not so great.
Square tower, carved upward by the laboured thought,
The imagined bare concept, how must that soften
Now to the ivory glow and pride unsought—
Queenly Andromeda not so exalted often.

TO GLOUCESTERSHIRE

To my own County where I was born, and the earth
Entered into my making and into my blood—
Which I praised better than any ever of Her birth,
(The City of Gloucester finding in me Her true mood.)
Where Southey only of the great makers was born
And I beat, because of the love of Earth in me—
He desiring books, and I truth rather than the
Writing continual—who saw Cotswold glorifying God,
And the eastern stars, pale out under the paling morn.
And saw Andromeda a sky wonder over Tewkesbury—
And praised Gloucester, and Tewkesbury and Brimscombe so
In all their centuries no man from any century.
And after making—with small chance—with no late working,
Came to London Town which was worse, and to be
Only comforted by the Thames dusk and the City dawns—
The stars of night and the paled East hour-pass marking.
(To lose heart, and health, a night walker's soul to electricity)
Who served in trenches as many a famed soldier
Unfamed of Caesar's Legions never had served—
Having read Plutarch now, and known the bolder
Lies of Historians—Whose spirit there never swerved—

AFTER WAR

One got peace of heart at last, the dark march over,
And the straps slipped, the warmth felt under roof's low cover,
Lying slack the body, let sink in straw giving;
And some sweetness, a great sweetness felt in mere living,
And to come to this haven after sorefooted weeks,
The dark barn roof, and the glows and the wedges and streaks,
Letters from home, dry warmth and still sure rest taken
Sweet to the chilled frame, nerves soothed were so sore shaken.

THE BARE LINE OF THE HILL

The bare line of the hill
Shows Roman and
A sense of Rome hangs still
Over the land.

So that one looks to see
Steel gleam, to hear
Voice outflung suddenly
Of the challenger.

Yet boom of the May-fly
The loudest thing
Is of all under the sky
Of the wide evening.

And the thing metal most
The pond's last sheen
Willow shadow crossed
But still keen.

How long, how long before
The ploughland lose
Sense of that old power,
The winds, the dews

Of twice ten hundred years
Have dimmed no jot
Of Roman thought there, fears
Triumphs unforgot.

Has Caesar any thought
In his new place, of lands
Far West, where cohorts fought
Watched at his commands.

Carausius, Maximus,
Is all let slip, then why
Does Rome inherit thus
Dominate memory.

So royally that Here
And Now are nothing known
The regal and austere
Mantle of Rome is thrown.

As of old—about the walls
Of Hills and the farm—the fields.
Scabious guards the steeps
Trefoil the slopes yield.

THE ELEMENTS

A writer thought, 'How lovely to rise and lave
My smooth fair body with water clear from earth drawn.
Ponder on it, and dig the garden, so little garden,
Drink tea, and smoke, write, thanking my Aunt's kindness
(Hoping to return work chance and all, as doubtless
I did—a friend of mine, and beyond thought kind
Often . . . . .) It was a chance of work past my hopes, save she
Would force tea, and trap to food, so it was terror to me.
So I'd go walking by Cotswold streams set a-talking
By a short course and steep from hills azure, green
Through the hawthorn hedges, and orchards dimly seen,
There by Haw Bridge and Forthampton, and the hill whose name
Is gone from me—where the silver brook earth bore and
                                          laughed silver,
By the landslide, to Hartbury, Maisemore and so where I came.
(To see Great Peters like Leonora over Severn meadows).
To talk and work, returning courtesy with company,
Till she'd go upstairs, then no more talking in lamp shadows
Golden and black on gold, I'd work hours untold
Reading Goethe and Shakespeare, seeing Longford meadows,
And getting notes on paper, and verse square bold,
Till the days tardied out over Kingsholm, and light soaked up
                                          gloom,
Quartettes and tea, tobacco, Elizabethans—none better of those.

My Aunt would come down fresh cheeked for all her years,
To find me writing, and I'd smile and talk my thanks,
Lie down, covered with a rug for one hour, with eyes clear,
                                        as on high Cotswold there'.

'Girl, girl, why look you so white?
        Is it death has you taken?'
'No, no, you must not question me so,
        Out of the air is this shaken'.

'Sickness out of the air can be cured
        By simples or one night in the open
But on you — heart's threat so as you stared
        Some power for you bad forelooking has shapen.'

'It is my dead love, who whispers me now
        I loved him well. I love you far better
That is not borne; anger, hurting, and scorn,
        I can take, but not to be of Love the debtor.'

'Yes, but for my love of him, he has called
        Me to his side, quick as maybe.
It was never so — it is lies; so enthralled
        Never I was, whate'er days tale be.

'My own heart's master I was and he
        The taker of what I spared
Out of the richness of my fancies (much less
        Of his worth) I dared.

'Shall the dead leave the deep clay to mind
        The living of a love year covered?
Does Death presume so? And out of the blind
        World of spirit a known one hovered.'

'Dear, let deny your heart, come kiss
        That past love out of fancy until
He as the morning mist on our hill
        Of delight be, bathed in sun bliss.

'Dear, let the dead one let you rest.
My heart is as rich with earth's love
Loving with poetry from the upturned fresh
Ploughland, with small weeds above.

'He had no more—let the terror slide out
(Of your eyes and heart) I too, beloved
Of earth—have such right of
Honour of the soul, delight of
Earth, you should be moved.'

'Though your girl's virginal naturalness
To the secretest wood be dear
(Or the ploughland) there are gods shall confess
I, too, the poet, have right here.

'May and September, the clear, the romance—one
Put fear away
That you have unfaithful been or looked deathly . . . .
To the earth's yea or nay.

'Only put out the blind terror from your eyes,
For one by dear earth chosen
For service, poetry, and love's ways
Of reward for service and for night seeking.
Wandering to music's heart after the day's
Common wonder (but never losen)
The common wonder of wandering and making.
Make love for me your solace for eyes
Feared awhile, and be calm to admire and see
There's evil in death does so awaken.

ALL SOULS DAY 1921

The smell of the earth there in the coloured plain
The bell tolling summons through colour and soft
Mist of clean air, and other land memories again.
These were of All Soul's Day indeed, and the loft
Of farmstead should have scented with sweet apples plain.

The shine there, Tuscan of look at corners round
Would have persuaded any to some acquiescent
Admiring of that faith grown in with the ground,
The earth itself with first worship grown-in and blent
Centred with hollow iron, in dark sound.

And the Autumn darkness good, as if Autumn had cast
By purple crocus there and trefoil a shade.
Not now the tea-time comfort to expect at last
No end of clean-walked body in rest laid,
The Times were not of making, but swift terrible waste.

But, O, the worship that hurt my heart with fear . . .
Going into the Merville Church, and seeing the bowed
Supplicating women with souls crying dark-deep to where
God might pity France again, and lift off the plague's
                                                    cloud . . .
And the mothers of the Dead by Robecq under bright
                                                    poplar.

BETWEEN THE BOUGHS

Between the boughs the stars showed numberless
And the leaves were
As wonderful in blackness as those brightnesses
Hung in high air.

Two lovers in that whispering silence, what
Should fright our peace?
The aloofness, the dread of starry majesties,
The night stilled trees.

WILLIAM BYRD

Friend of Ben Jonson, or if not friend, equal
In his great strength, but with tougher and less plastic
Material — and no instruments like to the English sense
Of words to use .... Byrd master and squarer of sound.
Well I remember walking down Farringdon Road
Finding the well printed loose binded Book inch thick —
And hastily fumbling for the shilling charged — a shilling was all.
And going home working, occasionally scanning
The noble words, music not yet truly found:
In my own work in middle night glancing for rest
At the five part or six part Motetts — to be stirred
By nobleness of look and music — and mind made sound.
To wonder, and to accuse Time of having withheld him from me
                                                        — opprest
By certain disliked things of old praised Palestrina.
Joyed by loved things praising loved Gloriana.
That page and this shape ....
And to walk at night and to guess how he too walked
Musing on Thames' look or talking late night
With Jonson or with friends of Jonson or Heywood ...
Greeting apprentices honour'd, the honoured master
Of Organ and singer — to God's praise giving delight.
Or merchants saluting courteous in midday mood ......
To wonder where he was born, honoured William Byrd ......
In what woman the desire for more life grew faster,
Where what loins in whom the life seed fell and stirred
(For thought of comradeship with Warwick and Hertford)
And what Church blessed with a cross that infant forehead ...

O glory that shape to square the shapes wondering;
O courage that makes the dumb spirit to submit and sing ...
O age of Greene and Shirley, Ford and Christopher
(That young one) beloved for airs at the difficult wicket
Swiping over the boundary with accustomed swing .....

What boys must have passed under that clement mastery;
Loved, and let the opportunity pass over.
To tell his conversations, and how he looked;

What tried for them the Chapter would not have liked;
Mid all up; and wrote till nights veil was nothing—
Square and the human beauty, proving and proving . . . .
Winter and first April and loved October,
Firelight or candlelight—that music sober.
After long talking with friends at the Day's ends;
Such friends as Gloucesters were to me in France; now,
By some imagined lost, but the natural friendliness
Of such as know the days twentyfour hours moving;
And on with wine till labour some high glory sends;
Some 'Such I would have' no less. . . . .
O Byrd, London lies a filth very low and low!
Could your great spirit clean it, she would be happier . . . .
But to all Christian purpose she is hog-slow
And for the dead, honours with graven stones and ceremonies.

HAD I A SONG

Had I a song
I would sing it here
Four lined square shaped
Utterance dear.

But since I have none,
Well, regret in verse
Before the power's gone
Might be worse, might be worse.

THE MOTETS OF WILLIAM BYRD

Nobly I saw them first
On great paper black printed . . .
And their strength showed, and more
Behind yet hinted.

It was in Farringdon Road
On a dull Day of London weather,
Small money had I, the day
With me, poor together.

After first puzzling glance,
The friendlier and comprehending . . .
Greatness showed from the page,
Mastery, square shaping.

Till my most critical
And searching spirit could not
Resist. 'How much' I turned and said,
'How much? Not a lot?'

It was only a shilling and
My heart sprang higher to be found
In company of the great friends of Jonson,
The makers of that old ground

On which I stood, for long
Had doubted more than worthiness
And beauty to the madrigals,
Not starkness, not greatness.

And I thanked. 'This book is
What I have long sought. Palestrina
Is lesser than this great strength is
A mystic, a dreamer.'

And talked of Missa Brevis
Praised Wilbye, Morley and others —
With greedy heart fears it be taken:
And envious fear smothers.

GLOUCESTER

Many have praised dancers
As folk of fine pride—
And I have seen foreigners
Dance, beauty revealed.

But on sombre ruddy
Lit lands of Gloucester—
Suddenly in March, suddenly
Gold princesses were master.

Of lovely and emerald lit fields
Winter saw desolate ..
They sang to far hills melodies
Like Easter water in spate.

They were like young children come
To a century-lonely house—
Heralds of a glory should soon foam
And glitter beside the hedgerows.

THE DANCERS

The dancers danced in a quiet meadow
It was winter, the soft light lit on clouds
Of growing morning—their feet on the firm
Hill-side sounded like a baker's business
Heard from the yard of his beamy barn-grange.
One piped, and the measured irregular riddle
Of the dance ran onward in tangling threads,
A thing of the village, centuries old in charm,
With tunes from the earth they trod, and naturalness
Sweet like the need of pleasure of change.
For a lit room with panels gleaming
They practised this set by winter's dreaming

Of pictures as lovely as are in Spring's range..
No candles, but the keen dew drops shining,
And only the far jolly barking of the dog strange.

OLD TAVERN FOLK

Five feet ten and fond of the sea, and glad
To sit the night through drinking, making merry,
Talking infinite sea yarns and widest like-things,
Till dawn stole in and showed masts, ships and wide
Headlands stretching outwards into gray mists.
They knew their craft and all such things as English
Might care for, thickets of interest like the masts
And spars of the swaying harbour-crowd outside,
Hugh, Michael, Nicholas, Sargeant and Barthelemy,
There was no craft nor hid thing but they had a touch
Of it and could smooth or touch a man on the rough:
Lies were a start of irony, only honour could
Hide its sight, or let loose what honour could hide.
Their dawns reached out to sights of all scheming Europe,
Name led on to name, they knew difference and every land's
                                                    hope,
Drank the last time and went to their untired business
Getting the honest good of life with the largest scope.

THE WOOD OF AUGUST

The wood gathers strength of green in mid August
Calling from the deep all store of April water
And later, to be triumphant while the time serves;
Golden rod, orchis, guilder rose and scabious
Grow near him, and he watches the three swerve
Of Cotswold Edge, South Severn and Malvern Sideways.
Soon he will change, the nuts will ripen, and tideways
Turn greater to the equinox, and brown and brittle
His leaves save the little will change, and he'll dream
Of two things: how in rich music is fixed his glow:
(Ruddy and bronze), and in All-Hallow his August title
With vanished days to it, is held as high as any
(Poor un-named English Company)
That haws last through November and dare winter's battle.

IMPROVISATION

City of my delight in the water meadows
Though they grime history and change all colour grey
Yet will a thousand memories of Europe's cities
Strive to guard you—yes, though even as they
Arthur and Guinevere you fall to soft renown,
But even so, with bad heraldry they cover high realities
In a thousand ways bond that should not feel one
You are held serfwise—and if from your light or skies
You would clear your heart or brow, they hide those over . .
Nothing earth's helps, shallow Severn, jagged countryways.

But, though the music or poetry in your name
Was done (for ages, ages by your renown called out),
Withers and is lies, destroyed, and is of evil fame,
Yet that is only part of a whole unsurpation;
None doubts but that kings and masters have had exaltation

High as the swerve to East in Cathedral and Hall,
Nor that Gloucester trumpets first rattled out Shakespeare's
fame
As a thing achieved. (The pools were glad of the rhythm).

Nor that all England travelling to Wales or Severn
Desired that to fairer Westminster a new foil might be given
More riches everywhere but chiefly here
A ford of army and market music and poetry's contest
That had the overlordship of Frome and of Avon,
These things are not doubted, the greater that all smooths out
Has not yet ground out faith in Arthur—and a million.

In December the stubble nearly is
Most loved of things
The rooks as in the dark trees, are its friends
And make part of it.

Now when the hills shine far
And light, and set off
That darkness, all my heart cries angrily
That music to fashion.

For if not so, one must go
To the stubble every day
For comfort against such emptiness
As lost treasures make.

Cruelly scare the choughs from
Fallows and trees alike,
Though dim in love, or bright far
With the hills heroically they ally.

MOMENTS

I think the loathed minutes one by one
That tear and then go past are little worth
Save nearer to the blindness to the sun
They bring me, and the farewell to all earth.

Save to that six-foot-length I must lie in
Sodden with mud, and not to grieve again
Because high Autumn goes beyond my pen
And snow lies inexprest in the deep lane.

The old walnut the children have loved so long
Must come down, the Squire needs a fine furniture,
Having things of honour, a chest and other
Must hold music, pictures of the land for
The land made, and after death the tree
May be more honoured yet than in greatness
There by the lawn, showing the red brick wall.
But in this November yet there is none to take
Truly its place but no monarch-show
Undoubted of one field's demesne.
His sons and daughters will grieve not after a little
But follow duty, and the children will climb them
As honouring and friendly. True the sweet music
Drawn out of the chest will sound there, and
Hospitality come.

SONG

Sing in me now you words
That she may know
What love is quick in me,
O come not slow

Not cold to me, but run
Molten, fiery-hot
Before Time soulessly
Make me forgot,

Or dull of image in
My dear Love's mind
You words, of power of flame
Be kind, be kind.

WOOD GATHERING

The gatherer will not go too far,
For fear of taking too much store,
But picks the bits of branches there
Where they lie, and looks at hills the more.

Returns, and who cares if the flare
Does not burn deep against the frost
So merry most-brave heat does stare
Against the folk, and roar up there.

When dusk veils all, they'll heap the spare
And noble wood, heap on heap without care,
For the noble frost will call for such cheer
Shining in white stars most royal in air.

I WOULD NOT REST

I would not rest till work came from my hand
And then as the thing grew, till fame came,
(But only in honour) . . and then, O, how the grand
Divination of ages grew to faith's flame.
Great were our fathers and beautiful in all name,
Happy their days, lovely in considered grain each word,
Their days were kindness, growth, happiness, mindless.

I would not rest until my County were
Thronged with the Halls of Music; and until clear
Hospitality for love were e'er possible . .
And any for honour might come, or prayer, to certain
Fondness and long nights talking till all's known.

Madness my enemy, cunning extreme my friend,
Prayer my safeguard. (Ashes my reward at end).
Secrecy fervid my honour, soldier-courage my aid.
(Promise and evil threatening my soul ever-afraid)
Now, with the work long done, to the witchcraft I bend
And crouch—that knows nothing good, Hell uncaring
Hell undismayed.

THE SHELTER FROM THE STORM

And meantime, fearing snow, the flocks are brought in.
They are in the barn where stone tiles and wood shelter
From the harm shield; where the rosy-faced farmer's daughter
Goes to visit them.

She pats and fondles all her most favourite first,
Then after that the shivering and unhappy ones,
Spreads hay, looks up at the noble and gray roof vast
And says, 'This will stop storms.'

Her mind is with her books in the low-ceilinged kitchen
Where the twigs blaze, and she sees not sheep alone
Of the Cotswold, but in the Italian shelters songs repeating
Herdsmen kind, from the blast gone.

This Christmas morning, once to the gods given,
We shall go sit amid stone where music wraps
Infinite cloaks companionable round people
That the dear Morning Star saw for sign of Christ.

Waking in our panelled rooms with no straw
And the content passion of Sebastian Bach
Soaring by clear and coloured windows to be
Heart of thought, this Christmas of clear shining.

The scent of that country is in many songs
Its desires are gone
On the winds of prayer and desire to the world's ends—
That Triumph, that has come.

So far that when men sing afar off
In any place of the world
Though they are labour's own, or earls of time's proof
Yet honour must give, and the word.

IN THE OLD TIME

In the old time when September's stubble gleamed
And as the content of all folk-writing seemed
The true consolation for all woes, I made
Music out of stubbornness and was glad.
But now the pen writes words, and the brain is content,
Fates haggle for me, the body has its bent,
And only theological and ethical discussions
Continue like a toothache, from black hidden dread.

THEN I HEARD

Then I heard a tramping in the winter leaves
And a knight rode from the clearing and stood beside
Me, this All-Hallows, silent with the day's pride
And reckoning. He looked on a thousand things,
Honour and honour again, villages and many cottages
Had borne the famous banner to where battle believes
True things of stolen record—lit up in murderous griefs.
Roland, Charlemagne, Arthur with silver sign
Blown to the mists, to the coppice-edges scattered . . .
He besides me, and of the chronicles speaking that
Were no more than ashes in the minds of men
Gone long withering gyring on careless soft breezes
With snatches of song, old earthy like his old russet
Jerkin—and weather coloured like his fine face.
The burrs on his legs, the drifted beech on his shoulders,
He praised the year's height, but I thought rather of
Long winter book evenings with the fire drifting on panels,
Books on the shelves, tobacco drifting, a friend talking
Shadowy all-hallowed memories drifting there.

TRAFFIC IN SHEETS

Silk colour and lit up candlelight the sheets I saw
By Severn Bridge that day . . . .
O, the lost history . . . O, ladies and pageants of the mystery
Of February here and miles away.

I could have sung, but knew no fitting tunes
(For all my lore) of the spread
Of coloured sheets of the floods that ensure all June's
Dark fan-grasses of the pretty head.

FRIEND OF THE MISTS

A thing of the field that loves the air between
And azure between gray branches,
Bird your own
You have that's known
With songs of romances
Of your age vast—
Unguessed age in a frosty morning
Known all green.
No word of the godlike
Beautiful, king, friendliest
Holy one that died . . .
Sing all in mourning phrases
Clear as the light in fruit-closes
The orchard tune sing with his own best . . .
Oath from all folk's lips
Save this strange one
Kept from his knowing.
O! the runes perished!
And dark days soon finished
And armour all tarnished
The last bird's silence.

DECEMBER 30TH

It is the year's end, the winds are blasting, and I
Write to keep madness and black torture away
A little—it is a hurt to my head not to complain.
In the world's places that honour earth, all men are thinking
Of centuries: all men of the ages of living and drinking;
Singing and company of all time till now—
(When the hate of Hell has this England's state plain).
By the places I know this night all the woods are battering
With the great blast, clouds fly low, and the moon
(If there is any) clamorous, dramatic, outspoken.
In such nights as this Lassington has been broken,
Severn flooded too high and banks overflown—
And the great words of 'Lear' first tonight been spoken.
The boys of the villages growing up will say, 'I
Shall leave school, or have high wages, before another January—
Be grown up or free before again December's dark reign
Brights them to Christmas, dies for the year's memory.'
May to them the gods make not all prayers vain.

Cotswold edge, Severn Valley that watches two
Magnificences; noble at right time or affectionate.
What power of these gods ever now call to you
For the folks in you of right noble; and of delight
In all Nature's things brought round in the year's circle,
Pray God in blasting, supplicate now in terrifical
Tempestuous movings about the high-sided night.

Men I have known fine, are dead in France, in exile,
One my friends is dumb, other friends dead also,
And I that loved you, past the soul am in torture's spite
Cursing the hour that bore me, pain that bred all
My greater longings; Love only to you, this last-year date.

THERE IS NOTHING*

There is nothing for my Poetry, who was the child of joy,
But to work out in verse crazes of my untold pain;
In verse which shall recall the rightness of a former day.

And of Beauty, that has command of many gods; in vain
Have I written, imploring your help, who have let destroy
A servant of yours, by evil men birth better at once had slain.

And for my Country, God knows my heart, and men to me
Were dear there, I was friend also of every look of sun or rain;
It has betrayed as evil women wantonly a man their toy.

Soldier's praise I had earned having suffered soldier's pain,
And the great honour of song in the battle's first gray show—
Honour was bound to me save—mine most dreadfully slain.

Rapt heart, once, hills I wandered alone, joy was comrade there
though
Little of what I needed, was in my power; again—again
Hours I recall, dazed with pain like a still weight set to my woe.

Blood, birth, long remembered, my County all these have saven
Little of my being from dreadfullest hurt, the old gods have no
Pity—or long ago I should have got good, they would have
battled my high right plain.

HEDGES†

'Bread and cheese' grow wild in the green time,
    Children laugh and pick it, and I make my rhyme
For mere pleasure of seeing that so subtle play
    Of arms and various legs going every, any, other way.

* Written February 1925 (in torture).
† Written at Dartford.

And they turn and laugh for the unexpensiveness
    Of country grocery and are pleased no less
Than hedge sparrows. Lessons will be easier taken,
    For this gipsy chaffering, the hedge plucked and green
                           shaken.

WHAT EVIL COIL*

What evil coil of Fate has fastened me
Who cannot move to sight, whose bread is sight,
And in nothing has more bare delight
Than dawn or the violet or the winter tree.
Stuck in the mud—Blinkered-up, roped for the Fair
What use to vessel breath that lengthens pain?
O but the empty joys of wasted air
That blow on Crickley and whimper wanting me!

WATCHING MUSIC

Watching music—guessing the sounds set down.
How on the real instruments they would sound, when
Gathered in a small room, lit with gold firelight thrown
Lovely about the room, the gloom riching again.
Strings should sound all man's heart ever found,
Or piano dearly touched tell truths tale of pain
Or Beauty . . . .". . . . .
                           Seeing the black
Notes on the page, cursing the sounds lack
To tell such imagination its true creation
To realise sound's beauty under the look

* 1. Written at Dartford. 2. *Poems of Ivor Gurney*, 1954.

Of crotchet, minim, quaver on the page,
So as to hear, as to the true musician's dear.
Shakespeare's words moving under the music—
Elizabethan clearness under the dumb sound,
Heart's-love to wound;
'Anthony' or 'Winter's Tale' moving under the fall
Or rise of sounding strings telling all out.
As a man to a woman will, when the first doubt
Of love accepted glows into love exalted.
('Beauty's ensign yet'—'Wilt thou be Lord of the whole
World—that's twice.'—and take the winds of March
With beauty'—'Girdle with embracing flowers—'
                              'My nightingale
In cradle of the rude imperious surge.'
All these things moving under like unknown names
Of deep love only spoken out by eternity's urge
Strings singing soft the hearts solace of grief,
Or exulting high forcing from weighted strings the belief
Of high Cotswold undaunted in morning sun.
Looking away past Severn and meadows of Uplead—
To surging Malvern or Welsh mountains by Brecknock known.
Night mystery, the unmatched glory of Orion.
Milky ways dazzle, on North East skies hazel
Or dark azure at midnight on dawn heralding on.
These things but music only spoken and under
Shakespeare's or Jonson's or some French poets equal wonder
Only in words told, not in music's gold.
These things of eternity, catching up to immortality.
Guessed in the trenches after ages of courageous cold.
Or on Cotswold walking alone, the God-chosen one.
Or the determined fray after Ypres Hell—battering day.
'This shall pay, I shall have music—music shall pay this pain;
Barrage, stray shrapnel, machine gun traverse and hurting
Terror of black danger, never ending, incessant starting.
Past men's bearing—this chosen for choice price . . . .
To hear strings tell out love's thoughts with tender voice
(O friends, O heart ache—dead are you or estranged.
God pity has changed
Towards me who was his worshipper, devoted server.

In all England I the one, I the one . . . .)
These black notes then, watching desperate out of my pain
To guess the content, to know what the maker meant
Realising such beauty, schooled to such discipline.
With equal art realising what dreams did make begin.
Black notes, to be moving arms, a bow on the strings,
Beauty matchless like twilights unfelt wings.
Or talk of Roman sentinels on the high Camps
Before are clean nights contemplative high aloof lamps.
These I should be playing with dearest friends in rooms
Lit with glooms, dark with firelight's gold power.
Taking pay for Laventie, or Vermand's hour.
Or of Ypres, Tilleley the complete terror.
Who, first was poet, am under three Hells and lie
(Sinned against desperately by all England high-sworn to
                                                    Duty)
Out of music, out of firelight—or any joy.
A tale of heroic courage, made pains mask.

SNOW*

There's not a sound tonight
I look out and am beaten
In my face by curious, white,
Unexpected flakes
Of snow in a daze fleeting.

And retire shivering to
The warm room and the lamplight,
Where my music waits, and O
Ben Jonson lies . . . .
To my delight my man's nature with his great spirit.

* Written 2nd January 1925.

O warmth! O Golden light!
O books behind me waiting
Their turn for my love's thought . . . .
Turning from work
To wrap myself in a past life of golden lighting.

Music must flow with his power, I
Bend over my task and am hard
At wrestling with the stuff for mastery
That is dumb music now—
My spirit and I wrestle, you may hear us breathing hard.

Was there ever any Love, could draw me
Out of my true way of work and action?
Yes, one there was, but Time has dared show me
(A soldier and maker)
That Time dares all things, and defies ever question.

THE TELEGRAPH POST*

The Telegraph post stands and is a foil
To the high and the dim sky,
Hardly aware of the ribbon of roadway
That's checked by it and then goes by.

But the poles on the edge of the rises out Westward
Are a symbol for all lonely travel
A strange distance of untold futures,
Significances hard to unravel.

* 1. Written at Dartord. 2. *Poems of Ivor Gurney*, 1954.

BACH—UNDER TORMENT

Lovely, brave, affectionate things they were,
Strong handled and sure touched to their strong end,
Protestant devoutness loved out all fear,
Youthful remembrance to a grown man still friend.
Artist of four strands, eight, with a hedger's deft
Sure-moving purpose, O, were that spirit to meet
In Europe's common-ways; the Father of great
And small since, would Time were, and storm had a rift.
O, will not Gloucester, nor Aubers, nor Ypres save?
I paid a price of love there could not be said
Anyway but huge of any thought of my sternest god.
Golden firelight or racked frost hurt me to the nerve.
O Bach! O Father of all makers, look from your hidden
Hold where you are now and help me, that am so hard hurten.

LOOKING UP THERE

'Hans Andersen', said the fir-tree
By the Roman farm buried,
And the flame worthy the hill-slope
Into heaven seem carried.

But the earth below with its coarse stuff
And reality and plain look,
Is better than other men's tales, and enough
To turn thoughts from any book.
How hard beauty hurts men with commonness and
       pangs and starts them!

THE LOCK KEEPER*

Men delight to praise men; and to edge
A little off from death the memory
Of any noted or bright personality
Is still a luck and poet's privilege.
And so the man who goes in my dark mind
With sand and broad waters and general kind
Of fish—and fox—and bird lore and walking lank,
Knowledge of net and rod and rib and shank,
Might well stretch out my mind to be a frame—
A picture of a worthy without name.
You might see him at morning by the lock-gates,
Or busy in the warehouse on a multitude
Of boat fittings, net fittings; copper, iron, wood,
Then later digging furious electric
Under the apple boughs, with a short stick,
Burnt black long ages, of pipe between set teeth,
His eyes gone flaming on the work beneath,
Up and down working like a marionette.
Back set, eyes set, wrists; and the work self-set.
Afternoon was of action but all nebulous
Trailed over four miles country tentaculous
With coalmen, farmers, fishermen his friends,
And duties without beginnings, without ends.

There was talk with equals, there were birds and fish to
                                              observe
Stuff for a hundred thoughts on the canal's curves,
A world of sight—and back in time for tea;
Or the tides change, his care, or a barge to let free.
The lowering of the waters, the quick inflow,
The trouble and the turmoil; characteristic row
Of exits and of river entrances,
With old (how old?) cries of the straining crews,
(Norse, Phoenician, Norse, British? immemorial use)

Tins would float shining at three quarter tide,
Midstream his line of fire, never far wide—
Dimples of water showed his aim to guide

* Poems of Ivor Gurney, 1954.

And ringed the sunset colours with bright ripples
Later, tide being past violence, his gates known safe
He would leave his station, lock warehouse and half
Conscious of tiredness now moving lankly and slow
Would go in a dark time like some phantom or wraith

But like a woodsman in a summer glow.
There he was not known to me, but as hearers know
Outside the blue door facing the canal path.
Two hours or three hours of talk; as the fishers know

Or sailors, or poachers or wandering men know talk.
Poverty or closing time would bring him again.
There was a width about the chimney corner,
A dignity and largeness which should make grave
Each word or cadence uttered or let fall save
When the damp wind in garden shrubs was mourner.
It would have needed one more well than I
To have questioned, to have pried each vain of his wide lore.
One should be stable, and be able to take wide views,
Have knowledge, and skilled manage of questions use.
When the captain is met, the capable in use,
The pictured mind, the skilled one, the hawk-eyed one
The deft-handed, quick-moving, the touch commanded one.
Man and element and animal comprehending
And all-paralleling one. His knowledge transcending
Books, from long vain searches of dull fact,
Conviction needing instant change to fact.
The nights in winter netting birds in hedges,
The stalking wild-duck by down-river sedges.
The tricks of sailing, the ways of salmon-netting;
The cunning practice, the finding, the doing, the getting,
The wisdom of every various season or light,
Fish running, tide running, plant learning and bird flight.
Short cuts and watercress beds, and all snaring touches,
Angling, and line laying and wild beast brushes,
Badgers, stoats, foxes, the few snakes, and care of ferrets
Exactly known and judged of on their merits.
Bee-swarming, wasp-exterminating and bird-stuffing.
There was nothing he did not know, there was nothing,
nothing.

Some men are best seen in the full day shine
Some in half light or the dark star-light fine.
But close in the deep chimney corner seen
Shadow and bright flare, saturnine and lean,
Clouded with smoke, wrapped round with cloak of thought
He gave more of desert to me, more than I ought—
Who was so used to books, so little to life.
One had seen the half height tides covering the sand
With purpose, cunning, creeping up, with silver band
But dark, determined, making wide on and sure.
So the man flowed behind his talk, to endure,
To perceive, to manage, to be skilled, to excel; to understand
A net of craft of eye, heart, kenning and hand,
Thousand threaded tentaculous intellect
Not easy on a new thing to be wrecked
Since cautious with ableness, and circumspect
In courage his mind moved to a new stand
And only with full wisdom used his hand.
Months of firelight and lamplight of night times before-bed
Revelations, a time of learning and little said
On my part, since the master was so wise
The lesson easy, and the grave night winds sighs
At window or up chimney incessant moaning
For dead daylight or for music or fisherman dead.
Dark river voice below heard and lock's overflow.

THE LOVE SONG*

Out of the blackthorn edges
I caught a tune
And before it could vanish, seized
It, wrote it down.

Gave to a girl, so praising
Her eyes, lips and hair
She had little knowing, it was only thorn
Had dreamed of a girl there.

Prettily she thanked me, and never
Guessed any of my deceit . . . .
But O Earth is this the only way
Man may conquer, a girl surrender her sweet?

BEHIND THE LINE*

I suppose France this morning is as white as here
High white clouds veiling the sun, and the mere
Cabbage fields and potato plants lovely to see,
Back behind at Robecq there with the day free.

In the estaminets I suppose the air as cool, and the floor
Grateful dark red; the beer and the different store
Of citron, grenadine, red wine as surely delectable
As in Nineteen Sixteen; with the round stains on the dark
table

Journals Français tell the same news and the great
Black printed columns give news, but no longer the moan
Of shrapnel or any evil metal torments.
High white morning as here one is sure is on France.

* *Poems of Ivor Gurney*, 1954.

TOWNSHEND*

Townshend? I knew him well, queer ways he had.
Fond of plays, fond of books, and of Roman talk,
Campments, marches, pila, and a mix of relics
Founded by Western folk in a casual walk.
A quick man in his talk, with eyes always sad.
Kind? Yes, and honourer of poets and actor folk.
Chettle and Heywood . . . but most Jonson he loved.
Angry with London for neglect that so evil proved
Who lived two years with him and was great labourer
As 'Cataline' and many other things to which he was moved
Showed; he read much Latin, and was proud of Greek,
Townshend would leave him whole days alone in his house
And go to Surrey or Buckingham and take delight,
Or watch Danbury changing in the March light.
Knowing Jonson labouring like the great son he was
Of Solway and of Westminster—O, maker, maker,
Given of all the gods to anything but grace.
And kind as all the apprentices knew and scholars;
A taker with battle honours till dawn whitened the curtains,
With many honourers, and many enemies, and followers.

There's one said to me 'I love his face,
But if he smites me flat for a false Greek quantity,
And drinks a quart where I should be trembler and shaker,
It must be said, "I love him". He does me disgrace
And I shall pay him back for the sigh of posterity
For all great Cataline and Alchemist its high play,
Unless he loves me more or I have greater charity.'

---

* 1. Aurelian Townshend. 2. *Poems of Ivor Gurney*, 1954.

NEAR VERMAND*

A park there, with a stream running, deep up-and-down
Banks sliding with green face, and young trees running hither
And thither in the small valley; up to the smooth crown
Of the steep; and we with full packs, weak with hunger,
Thought of the present labour with dull anger.
The copse was like a Cranham copse with scythed curve—
In a month violets would bloom, but no Birdlip swerve
Meet our eyes—Roman—backs turned to that far West
Where April is pattern of living not merely guest pressed.
And we were in forced marches after an enemy
Through snowstorms and such, seeking an end to this ending.
But an order took us, order. We were led, brought to the four
Ways of Vermand, at the station place, turned East to more
Digging, but new wood-searching, and new good war tricks
With Germans seen actually, and private bivouacs
(Rain-spoilt) and March stars spoiled with gray cloudy racks.
Winds are driving rain sheets in white deep lines over
Country to Malvern perhaps, but what use to that
Body which cannot be of spirit the mover,
And is still, when swift speed is its right to be at.
Clean life is round, wind in elms, driving glorious
To the night hills, when October is friendly and furious.

ROBECQ AGAIN*

Robecq had straw and a comfortable tavern
Where men might their sinews feel slowly recovering
From the march-strain, and there was Autumn's translucence
In the calm air and a tang of the earth and its essence.
A girl served wine there with natural dignity
Moving as any princess from care free,

* *Poems of Ivor Gurney, 1954.*

And the North French air bathed crystal the flat land
With cabbages and tobacco plants and varied culture spanned.
Beautiful with moist clarity of Autumn's breath,
Lovely with the year's turning to leafless death.
Robecq, the dark town at night with estaminets lit,
The outside roads with poplars, plane trees on it,
Huge dark barn with candles throwing warning flares,
Glooms steady and shifting pierced with cold flowing airs,
With dumb peace at last and a wrapping from cares.
'O Margaret, your music served me. I also made beauty.'

THE BRONZE SOUNDING*

In the old days Autumn would clang a gong
Of colour between Cranham and the Birdlip curve,
Hollow brass sustained the woods' noble swerve
And the air itself stood against music as crystal strong.
So it may be so still, but the body now
No longer takes in distance as slow thought,
Old man's beard may be tangled in black hedges caught,
But the body hurt, spirit is hindered and slow,
And evil hurts me past my maker's right.

THE NOT RETURNING*

Never comes now the through-and-through clear
Tiredness of body on crisp straw down laid,
Nor the tired thing said
Content before the clean sleep slumber the eyes . . .
Or ever restless rise

* *Poems of Ivor Gurney*, 1954.

Pictures of far country Westward, westward out of the sight of
Never more delight comes of the roof dark lit   [the eyes.
With under-candle-flicker nor rich gloom on it,
The limned faces and moving hands shuffling the cards,
The clear conscience, the free mind moving towards
Poetry, friends, the old earthly rewards.
No more they come—no more.
Only the restless searching, the bitter labour,
The going out to watch stars, stumbling blind through the
                                                    difficult door.

HORROR FOLLOWS HORROR *

Horror follows horror within me;
      There is a chill fear
Of the storm that does deafen and din me
      And rage horribly near.

What black things had the human
      Race in store, what mind could view—
Good guard the hour that is coming:
      Mankind safe, honour bring through.

THE HIGH HILLS *

The high hills have a bitterness
Now they are not known,
And memory is poor enough consolation
For the soul hopeless gone.
Up in the air there beech tangles widely in the wind—
That I can imagine.
But the speed, the swiftness, walking into clarity,
Like last year's briony, are gone.

* *Poems of Ivor Gurney*, 1954.

TOWARDS LILLERS*

In October, marching taking the sweet air,
Packs riding lightly, and home thoughts soft coming,
'This is right marching, we are even glad to be here,
Or very glad?' But looking upward to dark smoke foaming
Chimneys on the clear crest, no more shades for roaming,
Smoke covering sooty what men's heart holds dear,
Lillers we approached, a quench for thirsty frames,
And looked once more between houses and at queer names
Of estaminets, longed for cool wine or cold beer.
This was war, we understood; moving and shifting about;
To stand or be withstood in the mixed rout
Of fight to come after this. But that was a good dream
Of justice or strength-test with steel tool a gleam
Made to the hand. But barb-wire lay to the front,
Tiny aeroplanes circled as ever their work
High over the two ditches of heart-sick men;
The times scientific, as evil as ever, again.
October lovely bathing with sweet air the plain.
Gone outward to the east and the new skies
Are aeroplanes, and flat there as tiny as bright
As insects wonderful coloured after the night
Emerging lovely as ever into the new day's
First coolness and lucent gratefulness
Of the absorbing wide prayer of middle sight
Men clean their rifles insentient at that delight
Wonder increases as fast as the night dies.

Now up to the high above aeroplanes go
Swift bitter smoke puffs and spiteful flames,
None knows the pilots, none guesses at their names,
They fly unthought courses of common danger,
Honour rides on the frame with them through that anger,
As the heroes of Marathon their renown we know.

* The *London Mercury*, Vol. XXIX, No. 170, December 1933.

OLD DREAMS*

Once I had dreamed of return to a sunlit land,
Of summer and firelight winter with inns to visit,
But here are tangles of fate one does not understand,
And as for rest or true ease, where is it or what is it?

With criss-cross purposes and spoilt threads of life,
Perverse pathways, the savour of life is gone.
What have I then with crumbling wood or glowing coals,
Or a few hours' walking, to work, through a setting sun.

I SAW FRENCH ONCE*

I saw French once—he was South Africa cavalry
And a good leader and a successful, clever one to me.
A knight of Romance—for the knight of Veldt was about him
Who outwitted Boers—few could—who laid traps and got him.
Egypt and Aldershot—Commander of the Forces
And Mons Leader—and Ypres of the Worcestershires.
Now Captain of Deal Castle—so my book advises.
We were paraded for six mortal long hours of shoulders strain
And after hours of cleaning up of leather and brasses—
(O! never, never may such trial be on soldiers again!)
And it was winter of weather and bitter chill,
Outside of Tidworth on a barren chalk slope—Wiltshire Hill
Six long hours we were frozen with heavy packs—
Brasses cleaned bright, biscuits in haversacks.
At last horses appeared hours late, and a Marshal
Dismounted, our shoulders so laden we were impartial
Whether he shot or praised us—Whether France of the Line
Or soft fatigues at Rouen or Abbeville or Boulogne.
Slow along the ranks of stiff boys pained past right use
Egypt and Veldt—Ulster—Mons, Ypres came

* The *London Mercury*, Vol. XXIX, No. 17, December 1933. *Poems of Ivor Gurney*, 1954.

And none to shout out of Ypres or cry his name —
Hell's pain and silence gripping our shoulders hard
And none speaking — all stiff — in the knifed edged keen blast.
He neared me (Police used electricity) Ypres neared me
The praises of Worcestershires, Joffre's companion Captain he
Who the Médaille Militaire the soldier known of France wore,
Scanned me, racked of my shoulders, with kind fixed face
Passed, to such other tormented ones, pain-kept-in-place
To stare so — and be satisfied with these young Gloucesters
Who joined to serve, should have long ago seen Armentières,
As Ypres, but at least Richebourg or near Arras.
But they would not send — youth kept us rotting in a town
Easy and discipline worried — better by far over by Ovillers —
Or Béthune — or St Omer — or Lys, Scrape, those rivers
To keep a line better than march by meadow and down.
Chelmsford army training to bitterness heart turning
Without an honour — or a use — and such drear bad days
Without body's use, or spirit's use — kept still to rot and laze,
Save when some long route march set our shoulders burning
Blistered our heels — and for one day made body tired.

Anyway, on the chill slope we saw Lord French, Commander on the
     hill
Of short turf, and knew History and were nearer History
Soon for scarred France — to find what Chance was to be feared,
To leave those damned Huts and fall men in shell blast and shots.
To live belt-hungry — to freeze close in narrow cuts
Of trenches — to go desperate by barbed wire and stakes
And (fall not) keep an honour by the steel and the feel
Of the rifle wood kept hard in the clutch of the fingers, blood pale

The coming of French after freezing so long on the slope.
Tidworth was Hell — men got Blighties — at least equal hope.
This was March — in May we were overseas at La Gorgue —
And the Welshmen took us, and were kind, past our hoping mind —
Signallers found romance past believing of War's chance.
But the leader of Mons we had seen, and of History a mien,
South Africa and the first days, Mons, Ypres and between.

CHRISTOPHER MARLOWE*

With all that power he died, having done his nothing . . .
And none of us are safe against such terrible proving
That time puts on men—Such power shown—so little done . . .
Then the earth shut him out from the light of the sun.
All his tears, all his prayers to God, and Elizabethan loving
Gone to a nothing, before he was well of age—
Having seen Cornwall, perhaps visited a loved Germany,
Known all London, read in many a poet's page—
Brave and generous, braggart and generous in doing,
Poet born and soldier, sobering to his elder age;
The earth covered him, and wrought wood was his clothing.
'Tamburlane' half glorious, the 'Faustus', half victorious,
He left us, chief, an ache that a poet true of men,
Should be stabbed cold, like any mean half gallant frothing
nothing
Other men honoured, great ones made a tradition true,
But we curse luck for silence in manner various—
The courage and youth and virtue of Christopher Marlowe.

WHEN THE BODY MIGHT FREE†

When the body might free, and there was use in walking,
In October time—crystal air-time and free words talking
In my mind with light tunes and bright streams ran free,
When the earth smelt, leaves shone and air and cloud had glee.

Then there was salt in life but now none is known
To me who cannot go either where the white is blown
Of the grass, or scarlet willow-herb of past memory.
Nothing is sweet to thinking from life free.

* *Poems of Ivor Gurney*, 1954.
† 1. The *London Mercury*, Vol. XXIX, No. 171, January 1934. 2. *Poems of Ivor Gurney*, 1954.

WHEN MARCH BLOWS*

When March blows, and Monday's linen is shown
On the gooseberry bushes, and the worried washer alone
Fights at the soaked stuff, meres and the rutted pools
Mirror the wool-pack clouds, and shine clearer than jewels.

And the children throw stones in them, spoil mirrors and clouds
The worry of washing over; the worry of foods
Brings tea-time, March quietens as the trouble dies . . .
The washing is brought in under wind-swept clear infinite skies.

DRACHMS AND SCRUPLES†

Misery weighed by drachms and scruples
Is but scrawls on a vain page.
To cruel masters we are pupils,
Escape comes careless with old age.

O why were stars so set in Heaven
To desire greedily as gluttons do;
Or childish trinkets—may Death make even
So rough an evil as we go through.

EARLY SPRING DAWN‡

Long shines the thin light of the day to north-east,
The line of blue faint known and the leaping to white;
The meadows lighten, mists lessen, but light is increased,
The sun soon will appear, and dance, leaping with light.

* The *London Mercury*, Vol. XXIX, No. 171, January 1934.
† The *London Mercury*, Vol. XXX, No. 178, August 1934.
‡ *Poems of Ivor Gurney*, 1954.

Now milkers hear faint through dreams first cockerel make crow,
Faint yet arousing thought, soon must the milk pails be flowing;
Gone out the level sheets of mists, and the West row
Of elms are black on the meadow edge, Day's dear wind is blowing.

THE TOUCHSTONE*

What Malvern is the day is, and its touchstone—
Gray velvet, or moon-marked; rich, or bare as bone;
One looks towards Malvern and is made one with the whole;
The world swings round him as the Bear to the Pole.

Men have crossed seas to know how Paul's tops Fleet,
That as music has rapt them in the mere street,
While none or few will care how the curved giants stand,
(Those upheaved strengths!) on the meadow and plough-land.

ROADS—THOSE ROADS*

Roads are sometimes the true symbolical
Representations of movement in the fate of man.
One goes from Severn of tales and sees Wales
A wall against England as since time began.

Hawthorn and poplar call to mind the different people
That rule and had shaping of this land at their periods.
One goes from the Abbey to the smaller steeples,
There made worthy, and by tithe-barns, and all by roads.

Poems of Ivor Gurney, 1954.

Daylight colours gray them, they are stained blue by the April
Skies on their pools and Summer makes carpet of dust
Fit for the royal; Autumn smothers all with colour
Blown clean away by the withering cruel Winter's gust.

Roads are home coming and a hope of desire reached,
(There is the orange window at the curve of the dark way),
Whether by Winter white frozen or by Summer bleached,
Roads are the right pride of man and his anxiety.

FEBRUARY DAWN*

Rooks flew across the sky, bright February watched
Their steady course straight on, like an etcher's line scratched.
The dark brown or tawny earth breathed incense up,
I guessed there were hidden daisies, hoped the first buttercup.

The tunes of all the county, old-fashioned and my own
Wilful, wanton, careless, thronged in my mind, alone
The sight of earth and rooks made passion rise in my blood,
Far gleamed Cotswold. Near ran Severn. A god's mood.

Save that I knew no high things would amaze day fall
I had prayed heaven to kill me at that time most to fulfil
My dreams for ever. But looked on to a West bright at five,
Scarred by rooks in purpose; and the late trees in strife.

* *Poems of Ivor Gurney*, 1954.

A MADRIGAL*

Trees, men, flowers, birds, nuts, sing one choir
One madrigal shout far: scatter clouds with brass:
Scholars, leave your book folded, run, follow here,
Harvest is done, the year's high set in flower . . .
Michael and his armed press, Raphael, all chivalry here,
Echo beat the tympan of the woods, cry all clear—
Blast, bray, bellow deep sounds for the Master of the Year.

GENERATIONS*

The ploughed field and the fallow field
They sang a prudent song to me;
We bide all year and take our yield
Or barrenness as case may be.

What time or tide may bring to pass
Is nothing of our reckoning,
Power was before our making was
That had in brooding thought its spring.

We bide our fate as best betides
What ends the tale may prove the first
Stars know as truly of their guides
As we the truth of best or worst.

* *Poems of Ivor Gurney*, 1954.

I LOVE CHRYSANTHEMUMS*

I love chrysanthemums and winter jasmine
Clustering lichened walls a century old,
Ivied windows that the sun peeps in
When dawn an hour gone sees the level gold.
But for my love, Sweet William, snowdrops, pansies,
To else she is cold.

And all the host of tiny or mighty things
Scattered by April, daring autumn frost.
Or of man's hand scarcely her imaginings
Touch, being save to these three careless almost
And save to me. This knowing should I envy
Princes of proudest cost?

EPITAPH ON A YOUNG CHILD

They will bury that fair body and cover you—
You shall be no more seen of the eyes of men,
Not again shall you search the woodlands—not ever again
For violets—the wind shall be no more dear lover of you.

Other children shall grow as fair, but not so dear.
And the cold spirited shall say 'It is wrong that the body
Should be so beautiful'—O puritans warped to moody!
You were the true darling of the earth of your shire.

And all the flowers you touched, but would for pity not pick,
In the next Spring shall regret you and on and so on—
Whether you are born again your love shall not be done—
In the most wonderful April or October your spirit shall be
                                                    mystic.

* *Poems of Ivor Gurney*, 1954.

Dear body (it is an evil age) that so enclosed
So lovely a spirit, generous, quick to another's small pain:
Is it true you in the dark earth must be down-lain?
Are there no more smiles from you in the house, sunlight drowsed?

I must find out a love to console my hurt loneliness,
Forget your children's beauty in the conflict of days—
Until there come to me also the sweetness of some boy's
Or girl's beauty—a Western spirit in a loved coloured dress of
flesh.

POEM FOR END*

So the last poem is laid flat in its place,
And Crickley with Crucifix Corner leaves from my face
Elizabethans and night-working thoughts—of such grace.

And all the dawns that set my thoughts new to making;
Or Crickley dusk that the beech leaves stirred to shaking
Are put aside—there is a book ended; heart aching.

Joy and sorrow, and all thoughts a poet thinks,
Walking or turning to music; the wrought out links
Of fancy to fancy—by Severn or by Artois brinks.

Only what's false in this, blood itself would not save,
Sweat would not heighten—the dead Master in his grave
Would my true following of him, my care approve.

And more than he, I paid the prices of life
Standing where Rome immortal heard October's strife,
A war poet whose right of honour cuts falsehood like a knife.

War poet—his right is of nobler steel—the careful sword—
And night walker will not suffer of praise the word
From the sleepers; the custom-followers, the dead lives unstirred.

Only, who thought of England as two thousand years
Must keep of today's life, the proper anger and fears,
England that was paid for by building and ploughing and tears.

* *Poems of Ivor Gurney*, 1954.

THE HOE SCRAPES EARTH*

The hoe scrapes earth as fine in grain as sand,
I like the swirl of it and the swing in the hand
Of the lithe hoe so clever at craft and grace,
And the friendliness, the clear freedom of the place.

And the green hairs of the wheat on sandy brown.
The draw of eyes toward the coloured town,
The lark ascending slow to a roof of cloud
That cries for the voice of poetry to cry aloud.

SONNET TO J. S. BACH'S MEMORY†

Honoured Sebastian, that to many men
Has been the speaker of their deep honour—
You that have kept makers in fine manner
Beyond any, save Shakespeare—here again
One writes to praise thee; and for the Christian
Greatness, thy nobleness of strict banner,
Of grey metal, of truth of love's demeanour—
Page on page with the look and life of stone—

Europe gives thanks ennobling, Sebastian,
When Her heart touches thy praise. It is Her own
Hard and age-old virtue, out of prayer grown.
The aisles that fill with thunder, the height that thrills,
Most to thy name respond. And it is predestined
That by the chief gratitude men will make miracles.

* *Music & Letters*, Vol. XIX, No. 1, January 1938.
† 1. *R.C.M. Magazine*, Vol. XXXIV, No. 2, 1938. 2. Reprinted in the *Daily Telegraph*. This reprint differed in some details from Gurney's own version because the Music Editor altered the grammar. (Note by M. M. S.)

THE SONGS I HAD*

The songs I had are withered
            Or vanished clean,
Yet there are bright tracks
            Where I have been,

And there grow flowers
            For other's delight.
Think well, O singer,
            Soon comes night.

WHEN I AM COVERED*

When I am covered with the dust of peace
And but the rain to moist my senseless clay,
Will there be one regret left in that ill ease

One sentimental fib of light and day—
A grief for hillside and the beaten trees?
Better to leave them, utterly to go away.

When every tiny pang of love is counterpiece
To shadowed woe of huge weight and the stay
For yet another torment ere release

Better to lie and be forgotten aye.
In Death his rose-leaves never is a crease.
Rest squares reckonings Love set awry.

* 1. *Music & Letters*. Vol. XLX, No. 1, January 1938. 2. *Poems by Ivor Gurney*, 1954.

INDEX OF FIRST LINES